D1510930

Planning U.S.A.

Also by George Soule

LONGER LIFE

TIME FOR LIVING

IDEAS OF THE GREAT ECONOMISTS

THE NEW SCIENCE OF ECONOMICS

Planning

U.S.A.

by George Soule

New York / THE VIKING PRESS

Foreword

Nowadays it would be impossible to find an industrialized nation that does not practice some form of national economic planning. There are so many types of planning that only an encyclopedic work could describe them all in any detail. This book is intended to trace the development of central economic planning by government in the United States.

The notion prevailed until recently that there are only two kinds of economies: one in which the important decisions are made by privately owned business concerns which vie for the approval of purchasers in a free competitive market, and the other in which there is little or no private enterprise and an all-powerful government rules production, consumption, and prices. The first type is called capitalism, the second, socialism. The conclusion that was usually reached, especially in the period between the two World Wars, was that no nation can successfully adopt central economic planning without a revolution that destroys private enterprise, as did the Communist revolution in Russia. Both conservative businessmen and Soviet Communist leaders were likely to adopt this view, which is still orthodox in Russia.

Yet governments in nations that have not experienced proletarian revolutions have long played a large role in their respective national economies through such activities as taxation and public spending, monetary policy, control of the banking system, operation of institutions recognized as in the public domain, and regulation of foreign trade. The United States Government engaged in some of these activities from the very beginning, and it has never completely abandoned them, even in the era of anarchic business rivalry that followed the Civil War. Later, in World War I, it adopted central planning for the duration of hostilities. The economic policies of central governments have always assumed major importance during war, preparation for war, or return to peace.

The installation of economic planning in the Soviet Union in 1928 attracted worldwide attention to the subject, especially during the Great Depression, but that experiment has not been duplicated; even nations in the Communist bloc have adopted wide variations from the Russian model. The interest in the subject has been stimulated elsewhere by the varied experience of the nations concerned and by their various goals. Imperfections in the operation of traditional economies in the more highly developed nations have created a demand for more rational policies. Underdeveloped nations have wished to attain a rapid growth of production and consumption.

The possibility of planning has been advanced by the development of statistical records and analysis. In the United States, most of this has been supplied since World War I, and by such agencies as the National Bureau of Economic Research, the Federal Reserve System, and the Departments of Commerce, Labor, and Agriculture. But generations before this explosion of scientific knowledge concerning economic behavior, the United States Government had created institutions and adopted policies designed to affect the private business sector and improve the opportunities of its citizens.

In short, it would be difficult to describe the kind of central planning now employed by any one nation, or to understand how and why it came into being, without examining the history on which it rests. This book, therefore, is confined to an effort to explain the origins and nature of planning in the United States (with the exception of two brief sections on planning in the Soviet Union). The historical sources used are mainly three: *Prosperity Decade,* by this author, which covers the economics of World War I and of the 1920s (New York: Rinehart, 1947); *American Economic History,* by this author and Vincent P. Carosso (New York: Dryden, 1957); and revised excerpts from *A Planned Society,* also by this author, published in 1932 (New York: Macmillan). The two histories have many references to original sources, and *American Economic History* contains a full bibliography. Much of my knowledge of the relevant subjects is derived from research for contributions to *The New Republic*, of which I was an editor from 1924 to the end of World War II. During this period I talked with many in official positions and participated in the development of thinking concerned with central economic planning.

G.S.

To MALCOLM COWLEY, *with gratitude and esteem*

Contents

Planning U.S.A.

CHAPTER 1

The Organizing Man

The conservative-liberal and the Marxist philosophies share a number of the same errors in their analysis of social forces. They both oversimplify the motives behind the activities of individuals. They overlook a significant tendency in social evolution, and they minimize the leading idea which can eventually be depended upon to give meaning to our activities.

The classical economists, with their liberal background, assumed as a premise "the economic man." This man was like the atom, on the composition and activities of which the physicists built their theory of the nature of substances and of the changes which take place in them. In the same way the nature and activities of the individual economic man were supposed to determine the structure of economic society. His main impulse was supposed to be the desire for material gain. Leave the individual economic man free to follow this impulse, said the classical economists, and the best interests of everyone would be served. The more efficient competitors would survive. The consumers would get what they wanted most, at the lowest possible prices. The automatic adjustments taking place through the interplay of costs and prices would maintain a healthy equilibrium in economic endeavor. The mainspring of it all, which was indispensable, was the desire for profit.

The Marxian revolutionaries accepted the conception of "the economic man" in a disguised form. Everyone was in search of material gain. You could not trust anyone, under the regime of private ownership of the means of production, to do anything but seek profit. The chief difference between the revolutionaries and the classical economists was merely that the revolutionaries denied that this process was beneficial to everyone. Though it did serve the interest of the owners, it suppressed the non-owners. These persons, in turn seeking their own material advancement, would in the end dispossess the small minority of owners and transfer the ownership to themselves. They could not, of course, do this as individuals, but only as a class; hence common ownership would take the place of individual ownership. The emphasis of the Marxist revolutionaries, like that of the traditional liberals, has centered about the issues of profits and property.

But it is now a commonplace of the sciences dealing with human behavior that "the economic man" is a myth. Man seems to have, to be sure, a desire for gain, and under the capitalistic system the owners of productive property certainly do seek profits. But man has many other impulses as well. You cannot abstract one of his impulses, pretend that it is a complete man, and account for everything that happens in a large realm of human endeavor on the basis of that one impulse.

A favorite trick not only of economists but of sociologists is to posit one, two, or more fundamental instincts in man, and then to build a theory accounting for human behavior on the basis of those instincts. Granted the premises, most of the theories are logical enough. But how can we know that the premise is correct in any of the theories? What is the real nature of man? What instincts is he born with? What traits does he acquire from his environment? The study of these matters is a complex one, which conscientious psychologists have not mastered. What we do know is that any theory which emphasizes any one motive at the expense of the rest is almost certainly fallacious. It is much easier to study how men actually behave in specific situations than to say what moves them to do what they do, or what the result of that motive would be under different circumstances.

Any realistic study of the way men behave even in producing and using material goods must quickly reveal that they exercise traits and have habits which cannot be accounted for wholly on the basis of the profit motive. We produce and enjoy flowers from our gardens. This is more complex than any activity based on the desire for material gain. We enjoy the colors and shapes of the flowers; we like to decorate our houses with them; we want to imitate a garden we have seen; we crave, perhaps, the social approval which comes from having a well-appointed home; we are satisfied by the order and composition which results from good planning; we derive a sense of well-being from the feel of the dirt and the physical exercise of digging; we like to exercise discrimination in what we plant; we take pleasure in the exclusive distinction of having a flower that others do not possess; we experience an impulse to activity which must be employed in a meaningful and creative way; we must carry a process through from beginning to fruition. Similar impulses, and others as well, may be found in the behavior of men in almost any field of endeavor. The completely logical classical economist would be at a loss to account for the garden unless the flowers were raised to be sold.

Scientists are not moved primarily by the desire for profit; neither are artists. They have to live, to be sure, and in a commercial world they have to find some way to sustain themselves, whether by the sale of their products or by the sale of their labor, or by the ownership of something that renders them a living; but they find fascination in the work itself. And there is something of the scientist or artist in almost everybody.

The Ancient Habit of Planning

We cannot identify a single motive as the cause of human behavior. But there is a leading habit or trait observable in many forms of social and especially of productive endeavor, which exists independently of whether this endeavor is carried on for gain. We need not call it an instinct or a fundamental motive; what particular elements in the psychological nature of man make him act in this way we need not, for the present purpose, inquire. It is enough to identify the manner of behavior, and to see that it is widespread and deep-seated. This is the habit of planning and organizing the task and the social group. Without planning and organization, most jobs could not be done at all, and a progressive technique of work or play would be inconceivable.

The self-sufficient farmer, in the days before machinery included more than a few simple tools and when there was no mechanical power except that in the muscles of men, women, horses, and oxen, had to organize his operations with great care. He was surrounded by an external environment consisting of the nature of the land and the soil, the succession of the seasons, the climate and rainfall. He had a family that had to be housed, fed, and clothed. The requirements of the job before him demanded the apportionment of the land available among crops, pasture, and woodland, the maintenance of the necessary domestic animals, the sowing, cultivation, and reaping of the crops at the proper times. The several members of the family had to attend to their shares of the work, the women not merely cooking, cleaning, and serving as at present, but often spinning, weaving, and pursuing other handicrafts. Such a cooperative producing and consuming unit could not proceed at all without forethought and order.

Of course it is not true that each farmer had to face this problem as if he were the first farmer in the world. Agricultural customs and ways of living represent a gradual accretion over many generations, son learning from father and grandson from son. Changes were gradual, and planning was, in a sense, barely conscious. Nevertheless, the planning and the order were there— largely a social outgrowth, to be sure, but modified and improved in detail from time to time as a result of the observations and experiments of individuals. Any helpful change had to be made in connection with the whole organization of the group life; frequently it required alterations in many other details. If every member of the primitive farmer's family had been "free" to seek his own gain in his own way, they all would have starved.

In most agricultural societies, also, the farmer required a community made up of a number of families, and eventually a somewhat specialized community. There arose the local or itinerant shoemaker and tailor, the blacksmith, the sawmill and the gristmill, the tanner and the hat factory. Each one processed or exchanged the products of others. But since the market and the custom of each was rather strictly limited as to locality, the various members of the community were easily integrated with the needs of the whole. Only a few products were bought from afar or shipped abroad. There was little occasion to make more than could be consumed, or to make less, no matter what the product. Foresight on the part of each specialist was both necessary and easy.

The inventor and improver of machinery, too, was exercising the faculty of planning and organization. He was given, by the environment and by the work of his predecessors, certain devices like wheels and levers, certain sources of power, certain mechanical principles. He made new combinations of these, or improvements in the old ones. The objective was to do more work more easily. The ostensible motive may have been, in many cases, material gain. But the method was inevitably the better arrangement of existing materials and forces of production. By thinking far enough ahead, and establishing new routines in the handling of these factors, he could increase the wealth unit per labor unit.[1]

So it was with the organization of factories, of commercial houses, of canals and railroads, of means of communication. The growing technique of industrial life was a function of the planning and ordering faculty of man. It involved the coordination of materials and of persons to accomplish tasks which could not be accomplished with more primitive materials or by individuals. Nothing is more natural to man than this faculty, whatever the "motive" which may be supposed to prompt him to exercise it. Man is rarely more at home than when he is so at work. And he is distinctly not comfortable when he is faced with a troublesome situation which he cannot organize.

This same faculty of man is, moreover, the one which admittedly produces the most far-reaching changes in his environment and his social customs. It is a truism that the widening of markets which accompanied the railroad, combined with the superior ef-

---

[1] James D. Mooney and Alan C. Reiley, in their book *Onward Industry,* discern a close analogy between a machine and an industrial organization. A machine is, they say, a mechanical example of coordination of effort. "The principle of leadership appears in that function of the machine which actuates all other functions, and, in a mechanical sense, delegates these functions. Even the mechanical equivalent of the staff principle appears in the safety valves on steam boilers, and the indicators of various kinds on many different machines, and often several on the same machine, all of which render an informative and advisory service. Of this the instrument board on an automobile is an excellent example."

ficiency of production which arose from steam power in factories using machinery, was what destroyed the handicraft, the local mill, the self-contained community and the self-sustaining farm. It built many of the great cities, deprived others of importance, brought about agricultural specialization, widened the employer-employee relationship. Our present civilization is better described as a machine or a technical civilization than as a capitalist or a profit system. Desire for gain existed long before the flowering of the industrial revolution. The institutions of privately owned capital and profit were characteristic of many earlier trading communities, regardless of their primitive methods of production. The profit motive is not the sole determining cause of what we have today. Our civilization is built upon, and wedded to, machine technique. And that, in turn, is too narrow a term for what is really a faculty of planning and organization applied, with the aid of the discoveries of science, to the production and exchange of goods. Though we ought to learn from the mistake made by the classical economist in attributing everything in the economic world to one trait, still we may, as a device to dramatize this idea, substitute for the "economic man" of the classical economist, the "organizing man."

Technical change did not begin with the industrial revolution, nor did it stop there. It had gone on with accelerated pace. So far, its possibilities seem to be boundless; every discovery and invention breeds ten new ones. And just as the fundamental changes of technique of a century ago remade the face of civilization and altered social customs, so the new changes are repeating the process and must continue to do so. This is why, when conservative-liberals talk about the regime of liberty and individual enterprise established by our colonial forefathers, they are talking about a phantom society which never did exist precisely as they picture it, and only vestiges of which survive today. And this is also why, when the revolutionaries talk about the "capitalist system" as something which is essentially the same now as it was when Marx wrote about it, and as something which can be changed only by the accession to power of a submerged class, they are talking about an abstraction which omits most of the shape and color of the reality.

The capitalism of today differs more from that of 1848 than the civilization of Soviet Russia differs from that of the capitalist United States. In the faculty of mankind which habitually so plans and organizes that technique is altered, we find the inevitable force of social evolution, the basic course of change.

The fact that the scientists and technicians do not now manage society—though they have been playing an increasing part in management—and that they do not produce the end results which they seek, or might seek if they thought more about it, is not contradictory to this statement. Nor does the fact that society as a whole is chaotic, and negates much of the beneficent possibility of the industrial organization which we have so far built up. The scientists and technicians do not monopolize the ordering faculty; for the most part they have concentrated their endeavors on highly specialized departments of its application. The faculty of planning and organization has not completed its job; it has scarcely begun that stage of its work which would be necessary if the world community were to operate in as sensible a manner as the early New England farming community. All we have said is that the same sort of habit which has been observed in the past ordering smaller areas and endeavors, planning, changing, and improving them, can be counted upon to attempt to bring order out of the chaos of the new world community. This impulse is irrepressible; whatever obstacles or groups stand in its way are bound in the end to suffer for their obduracy. It will burst up through the crust of custom and eventually scatter any hampering traditions. The ideas and activities which it embodies have a universal appeal; its processes are those which the most active and intelligent delight to exercise in some realm or other. They will lend strength to any group, party, or class which espouses them. But the trait of organizing, not the particular instrument of its accomplishment in any special case, constitutes the "prime mover" of social change.

The Role of Leadership

Though the "organizing man" may give us the reliable force of change for which we are looking, and though the result of his activity may be, in a broad sense, an inevitable trend toward world order, still it is important not to rely upon him as an automatic force outside ourselves, or to rest in mystic assurance of "progress" that is undistinguishable from the shallow optimism of the years before the First World War.

So obvious a fact as the organizing faculty has led to many studies of the phenomenon, from which it is possible to learn a great deal concerning the modes in which it may be expected to operate. One of the first observations to be made is that social organization, even of a fairly complex nature, is a primitive human characteristic; anthropologists have encountered it everywhere and have portrayed it in large numbers of variants. It does not, in its more primitive forms, appear to be a reasoned activity. Nor is it, in these forms, highly flexible. Its preservation rests on habit and tradition; in turn it molds the habits of the tribe or people who practice it. Each form of organization has developed over a long period of time. It includes practices which appear to be the outcome of a process of adaptation to the environment; they have a biological value. It includes other practices which appear to have no material usefulness, but rather are aesthetic or religious in nature. It sometimes includes practices which appear to be biologically harmful. Anthropologists have been divided as to whether these cultures arose spontaneously or were learned by diffusion from common centers. But at least there is good reason to believe that imitation of other cultures has played a large part in cultural establishment and change.

Introduce an important new element, such as machinery, into the habits of a primitive people and the culture pattern adapts itself only with supreme difficulty to the new situation. Often the old culture pattern is destroyed; nothing equally organic takes its place; and the tribe in question degenerates, though retaining stubborn survivals of its old habits. The original pattern was not planned in its entirety; it arose slowly and rested on entrenched habits which were justified in the minds of the people who practiced them, in so far as they were justified at all, by mystic or religious absolutes of belief. Hence the pattern could not readily be altered to cope with a drastic change in the environment.

Many survivals of primitive culture are found in modern organizations. Secret societies built about "mysteries" and proffering fancy costumes, plus the distinction of an assumed superiority or exclusiveness, go back to primitive origins. The gang in the city, which starts with the grouping of boys about a leader and often ends by becoming a band of gunmen exploited by dope rings, politicians, or racketeers, is an expression of the need for group action and leadership in a society which offers the city boys little other opportunity to satisfy this need.

One widely observed principle of social organization is that, whether or not a given group formally accepts the method of majority rule, its main activity centers about, and is carried on by, a minority. The minority may consist of a single leader or a relatively small number of persons. But here originate the driving force, the direction of activity, the formulation of concepts about which popular emotions center. The political machine which runs the government is such a minority. You will see the same process at work in any club, society, or committee. The activities of trade unions are carried on by a few leaders and active members. In the world of ideas or letters, new schools or conceptions originate with one or a few persons, and gradually percolate to a wider audience. Successful revolutions arise from the work of cohesive minorities, who are more active, intelligent, and daring than the general public. Soviet Russia has made an accepted and disciplined institution of the political machine, by means of the Communist Party, a carefully selected minority group whose boss is the real and acknowledged ruler of the country, and whose members provide the leadership in every locality and factory.

Successful leadership of course implies acceptance of leadership on the part of the followers. It does not mean arbitrary rule enforced by penalties applied by the ruler. Leaders may employ such penalties, but unless the majority sanctions them in the interest of the group, the leader will not hold his power indefinitely. The principle of the leading minority does not imply autocracy in the ordinary sense; it simply means that every majority, if it is to be effective, must have an active center about which to coordinate its work and ideas. Universal suffrage and the rule of the majority vote are, in essence, a formalization of the principle that the group must have a leader whom it is willing to follow. If these concepts are understood to mean that leadership inheres in every individual of a group, and that the entire group must provide the direction and the ideas for itself, democracy is bound to be a tragic farce. Persons can be led; their activities can be coordinated; but they cannot be amalgamated except on a plane of primitive and unintelligent impulse.

There is nothing more destructive than an undisciplined and undifferentiated crowd, acting on the highest common denominator of its several impulses—which is bound to be an exceedingly low denominator. This does not mean that the members of the crowd are necessarily low fellows; it means that it is easier for them, under the stress of the mob spirit, to give rein to their more primitive impulses than to their reasoning faculty or their civilized inhibitions. Leaders who exploit the crowd by expressing nothing more than this highest common denominator, who adopt the easy way of following the crowd along the lines of least resistance, are the enemies of any fruitful principle of organization. Recognition of this truth is the source of the contempt in which are held such phases of crowd action as lynching mobs, self-seeking demagogues, or even the success accorded to "popular" and insincere forms of literature, art, or advertising which flatter and deceive the crowd for the quick material advantage of some minority. It is a good rule of thumb that a first-class novelist, playwright, scientist, philosopher, or social innovator does not find prompt acceptance with the majority. He is usually first understood and appreciated by a minority, and his reputation grows through their influence. In the end, however, he may provide far more profound and enduring satisfactions for people in general than some person who has the trick of attracting popularity.

The Unforeseen Results of Planning

As man's organizing faculty proceeds, its effect becomes more far-reaching. In its simpler forms, the development of technique may be conceived principally as a process of adapting human beings to their natural environment. Primitive man slowly changes his habits, his ways of working and fighting, in order to be more sure of getting food, clothing, shelter, ornament, and dominance over his enemies. But as technique develops it begins to change the environment itself. Man may kill off game. He may cut down forests. He may deplete the fertility of virgin soil. He may exhaust mineral resources. He may protect human life so well against enemies or disease that overpopulation ensues. Most striking of all are the tremendous changes in environment brought by mechanical power and machinery, and the organized activities which have sprung up to employ them. Within a few generations the face of the world and the type of problems with which man must deal have been radically altered. Not only does the organizing faculty change the environment, but it appears to change it at a constantly accelerated pace. Whereas earlier generations had centuries in which to adapt themselves to changes by slowly accreting or discarding habits, we have only decades.

It is clear that the organizing faculty usually produces not only foreseen, intended changes but others that are unforeseen and unintended. The intended changes appear to be advantageous: a railroad furnishes quicker transportation for longer distances; a new machine does more work with less labor. The unintended changes may be extremely troublesome: the railroad leads to overconcentrated metropolitan populations and slums; the machine produces unemployment. Automobiles not only furnish mobility to normal transport and travel; they also congest city streets, contribute to air pollution, and provide a ready means of escape for criminals. We deliberately adapt our habits as far as is necessary to produce the intended changes, but we usually do not adapt our habits readily to cope with the unintended changes. These come upon us as if some god had decreed them; we tend to regard them as a manifestation of fate and to hold as closely as we can to our old cultural pattern by way of defense against them.

This phenomenon has been given, by Professor W. F. Ogburn, the apt name of "the cultural lag." Developing technique and inventions rapidly produce a new environment; but the culture pattern fails to keep pace with technical change. It is bound by tradition, habit, and taboo; in this respect we are like the primitive races studied by the anthropologists. The vested interests of old or particularistic organized groups stand in the way of adaptation. The disparity between our old habits and the new environment creates increasing discomfort and danger; social strain is observable on every hand. Eventually readjustment of some sort comes. In the end it is usually the old culture pattern that breaks down rather than use of the new technique. Culture then changes by a sudden jump. This is what happens on a large scale when a social revolution occurs. It may also happen on a smaller scale or by a less violent change.

Another useful way to consider the effect of developing technique is to understand the change of scope which it presents to the organizing faculty. While handicrafts persist, the unit of production remains small, and hence small-scale organization is appropriate to deal with it, as on the self-sustaining farm or in the primitive tribe. But when machinery is invented, it makes the original process automatic. The organization inherent in the machine takes care, once and for all, of the coordination which formerly had to be exercised by human beings every time the operation was performed. The automatic reaper replaced the hand-swung scythe and the rake. The automatic loom does the work of the old skilled hand-weaver. And as machinery develops, it coordinates whole series of what used to be separate machine operations. The combine not only reaps but threshes automatically, turning out separately the grain and the straw. Machines in series, such as those found in steel mills, perform a whole train of operations without the intervention of a human hand, except that of the man at the levers and the buttons. Thus attention is released from the details of the automated processes. At the same time, however, there arises a necessity of coordinating the automated processes with one another. The combine makes economical the giant wheat farm. Machines, and especially machines in series, make necessary the substitution of the great factory or mill for the old shop. These large units must be organized. Furthermore, transportation, combined with large-scale production, has broadened markets and specialized all sorts of functions among widely separated establishments. The attention of organizers, once they have learned how a single factory or mill may be efficiently operated, is attracted to the organization of series and combinations of factories, to large financial matters, to the conditions of worldwide markets. The field wherein organization is necessary increases in area and complexity as organization reduces to automatic and learned habits the smaller tasks.

A final observation must be made before we concentrate these various beams of understanding on our central problem. In its primitive forms, organization of materials and men appears to be almost an unconscious activity. It arises by the slow growth and change of habits. Minor variations occur, either by chance, or by the ingenuity of an individual applied to a detail, or by the imitation of a practice found in another group. Culture patterns are passed on from generation to generation. Those habits which tend to increase the opportunity of survival for the group tend, by and large, to persist. Thus the process is virtually one of natural selection. This is sufficient when change of the environment is slow. But with the development of technique and the more rapid alteration of environment, there arises a more reasoned and conscious art of organization. It employs foresight and experiment. It attempts to outline a dependable science as a guide to its activities. This reasoned effort, this deliberate application of tested principles of organization, is the means by which man may cope with the exceedingly rapid changes accompanying the maturity of the machine age. And it must be applied to the whole array of changes produced by new techniques. We must inquire not merely what are the intended changes brought by a new device, but what may be the unintended changes. The area of the unforeseen must be restricted as narrowly as possible. Foresight must be employed in the interest of control and adaptation. This foresight and control is the instrument with which we may reduce the cultural lag. It is the embodiment of intelligence and will. It is the enemy of the vague, the complacent, the superstitious, the inert.

National or Social Planning

Planning, in the historical background of this book, does not necessarily mean the abolition of market forces, or the outlawing of private profit as a stimulus to production of goods and services wanted by consumers. Rather, it means influencing existing economic habits and outlook by a program which serves needs not contemplated by, and not normally fulfilled by, the existing order. National planning looks at wider horizons or longer futures than do the daily decisions of the managers of individual firms or industries. And its goals, if sanctioned by the citizens, make use of foresights and capabilities developed by the "organizing man," in the domain of a whole society. This concept will become clearer as we follow briefly the development of planning in the United States.

CHAPTER 2

Early Planning in the U.S.A.

In recent years we have come to expect that when a group of big manufacturing companies—among which price competition does not seem to flourish—is warned by the federal government to hold prices down lest inflation follow, their answer will be that "the market" can be trusted to adjust prices for the benefit of all. In so arguing they refer to the classical economic theory which Adam Smith, the shrewd Scotsman, elaborated in *The Wealth of Nations*. His book was published in 1776, the year when thirteen British colonies in North America declared their independence. Eleven years later, when the founding fathers met to adopt a constitution, they proved to be deeply impressed by Smith's reasoning, by his abhorrence of monopoly—a feeling they shared—and by the limitations he set on the types of action that he deemed appropriate for governments. Even then, however, the new federal government was prepared to engage in some forms of economic planning in order to serve the welfare of the nation.

What Adam Smith deplored especially was the policy known as Mercantilism, which was practiced at the time by France, Britain, and other European nations. A central aim of Mercantilism was to insure that the nation's exports were higher in value than its imports. The difference in value would be paid in precious metal, thus increasing the nation's hoard of gold or other "treasure." The citizens of that country could not eat the "treasure" or use it for any other practical purpose (except to finance companies which, by making profits abroad, could bring back still more gold and silver). As for the people of the importing regions (which included the American colonies), they not only lost the precious metals that they needed for currency, but also might be forbidden to export goods that would compete with the products of manufacturers in the "mother country." In 1750, for example, England had decreed an Iron Act which, though it sanctioned the production of pig iron and bars in the American colonies, where iron ore was plentiful, prohibited the manufacture of finished iron goods, since these would compete with English exports to the colonies.

Mercantilism had other vicious effects. At least in France, where it was known as Colbertism (after the great minister of Louis XIV who inaugurated the policy), it led the government to enforce low wages and long hours for French workmen, to forbid their emigration, and to obstruct the importation of grain even when famine threatened—all this because the foreign payment in "treasure" might thereby be diminished.

Adam Smith favored an opposite governmental policy toward economic production and trade, a policy that came to be known as "laissez faire." The French phrase might loosely be translated, "Don't interfere"—that is, with private enterprise. He had much to say about the diversity of competitive markets—how they arise from the nature of human beings and how men, if left to themselves, would most efficiently carry on their activities of production, sale, and purchase. He wrote that men alone, among all the animals, have an innate propensity to barter and trade: "Nobody ever saw a dog make a fair and deliberate exchange of one bone for another with another dog."

The basic means by which production is increased, Smith wrote, are the division of labor and the introduction of machinery. The output per worker is multiplied by specialization of operations, which in turn depends on a wide extension of the market, even though relatively few are engaged in the production of a given article. The market is widened by improvements in transportation, which thus facilitate the growth of commerce and industry.

The real value of any product depends on the labor required to make it. That labor is measured, Smith wrote, not merely by the amount of time required but also by the intensity of effort and the training or education of the worker. The effective demand for any article—that is, not just the desire for it, but willingness and ability to pay for it—may exceed the supply and so increase the price. Profitable sales would then invite competition, which would decrease the price. When demand and supply at any price are in equilibrium, that price is the natural one. Thus, everyone gains by a free market, since each obtains what he wants most at the lowest possible price. Obviously Smith regarded competition as an absolute necessity. "Monopoly," he wrote, "is an enemy to good management." Since land is limited, he regarded rent as a monopoly price.

As for the functions of "the Sovereign or Commonwealth"—his names for government—it must provide for national defense. But government must remember that industry is the essential basis for military strength and that it becomes continually more essential as weapons become more highly developed and expensive. Government must also dispense justice (although there must be an independent judiciary). Government should pay for the expense of public works advantageous to all, such as turnpikes and canals (of course there were no railroads at the time). Some of these improvements might charge tolls and thus become self-liquidating. Government might protect foreign commerce, but should not perpetuate monopolies or delegate armed defense to particular interests, as the British had done in the case of the East India Company. Government ought to subsidize elementary schools, and finally, as a matter of course, it must maintain the dignity of the sovereign.

Perhaps most remarkable of all for an author writing in 1776, Smith recommended a graduated income tax, of which "the time of payment, the manner of payment, the quantity to be paid, ought all to be clear and plain to the contributor, and to every other person." That quotation ought now be hung in the offices of the Bureau of Internal Revenue.

It seems likely that Adam Smith would have approved of many policies instituted by Alexander Hamilton, the first Secretary of the United States Treasury. But there were other policies of Hamilton that he probably would not have sanctioned, as notably a protective tariff and bounties to "infant industries."

Hamilton's Planning of Money

If an economy of any sort is to work well, it must have a reliable system of currency with which its citizens can carry on their transactions. The American colonies and their first Confederation did not enjoy such a monetary system. Until the Constitution was adopted, the new nation did not issue coins of its own mintage. Such specie or "hard money" as its citizens possessed consisted partly of coins issued by the several states and partly of those received from abroad—primarily Spanish dollars—in payment for exports. Coins were scarce. Of course in a modern economy they constitute a very small part of the total stock of money, but no dependable substitute for coins was in wide use during the immediate post-Revolutionary period. Banknotes were lacking for the simple reason that a banking system had not yet been developed. There were only three banks with charters granted by states when the United States became a nation. In order to carry on the Revolutionary War and to pay governmental expenses after peace came, the various states and the central government had issued paper bills and bonds totaling about $75 million. These could not be redeemed at par from governmental revenue, and inflation had drastically reduced their market value.

Among the most important clauses of the new Constitution were those which gave the Congress control over coinage, regulation of its value, and the power to levy federal taxes. After the Constitution had been ratified, one of the first acts of the Congress was to adopt, on September 2, 1789, a motion by James Madison to establish a Treasury Department with a single head, and to instruct its future Secretary to "digest and prepare plans for the improvement of the revenue and for the support of the public credit." President Washington promptly appointed Alexander Hamilton Secretary of the Treasury.

Hamilton's first two reports to Congress came so close together that it was obvious they dovetailed with each other as a plan for providing money for the use of the economy. The first, dated December 31, 1789, was a "Report on a National Bank," the second, on January 9, 1790, was entitled, "Report on the Public Credit."

The bank, which Congress eventually chartered on February 25, 1791, as the Bank of the United States, he regarded as the most flexible means of creating money, through the issuance of banknotes. The government retained a minority ownership of its capital; the Secretary of the Treasury received regularly reports on its condition, and retained the right to inspect its books and supervise its affairs. The government purchased $2 million of the bank's authorized capital of $10 million; the remainder was open to public subscription. The Treasury deposited the major part of the government funds in the bank without charging interest. The bank, in return, transferred about the country through its eight branches the money received by the government or paid out by it. The bank retained ample specie reserves, issued notes for $5 or more, which circulated freely throughout the nation, and redeemed in gold or silver any of its notes presented for redemption. The Treasury accepted its notes for the payment of taxes. Among other services, the bank played a large role in financing foreign trade, through handling foreign exchange and collecting import duties for the government.

The Bank of the United States (BUS) was in a position to discipline the growing number of banks chartered by the various states. It normally accepted their notes. If, however, inflation was threatened, the BUS would present such notes to the issuing banks for redemption, thus checking their ability to lend. It could put out of business any bank which could not or would not redeem its notes in specie, by refusing to accept those notes from customers.

The BUS made loans to the Treasury, but it did not wish to lend so much as to curtail its loans to other borrowers. In 1802, Secretary of the Treasury Gallatin repaid the outstanding loans from the bank by selling the government's stock, thus making a capital gain of $700,000, or 30 per cent of the original investment.

Naturally a bank with such power made enemies, and in the eyes of Jefferson's Democratic Republican Party it represented too much central control. When its twenty-year charter came up for renewal in 1811, Congress defeated the bill—but only by a vote of 65 to 64 in the House of Representatives and a tie of 17 to 17 in the Senate. Without the BUS, speculative inflation and many bank failures occurred just before and after the War of 1812. The wholesale price index (as estimated many years later by the Bureau of Labor Statistics) rose from 104.9 in 1811 to 154.6 in 1814 (1926 = 100). After this experience, and lacking any effective control of private and state banks, Congress established a second Bank of the United States in 1816, again with a twenty-year charter. Still later, however, President Jackson became an enemy of this second bank and prevented a renewal of the charter when it lapsed in 1836. This is not the place to summarize the long history of banking in the United States, but it must be added that the function of central banking—to stimulate economic growth without encouraging swings of inflation and deflation—was served more than a century later by the development of the techniques practiced by the Federal Reserve system.

The other major fiscal policy favored by Hamilton, and reported to Congress on January 9, 1790, was his plan to deal with the governmental debt of about $75 million, a huge sum for a time when the total population of the country was about 4 million. There was virtually no specie reserve behind the paper bills and bonds that had been issued by the states and the nation to finance the Revolutionary War. The purchasing power of these instruments had been rapidly approaching zero because of the rise in prices during the war. Hamilton's recommendation was a startling and courageous one. It was, in essence, that the new federal government should assume responsibility for all these instruments of debt, both federal and state, and offer to redeem them at par value. He might have advised that the national government buy them at their low market value. He might even have advocated repudiation of the debt. His actual plan, which was adopted, was that the federal government issue new obligations in exchange for the almost valueless bonds and bills, at their face value, that it pay a regular interest to the owners, and that the debt be retired in an orderly manner over a period of years. There could be no doubt that these measures would restore the original value of the paper money. Consequently, the money would add to the purchasing power of the citizens who held the instruments of debt—a quick way of providing capital which, it was hoped, would be necessary in developing the national economy. Unlike many subsequent conservatives, Hamilton saw no harm, but an actual gain, in the existence of a large national debt. "It is a well-known fact," his report read, "that in countries in which the national debt is properly funded, and an object of established confidence, it answers most of the purposes of money."

Opponents of Hamilton argued that bonds and bills had passed from the hands of their original recipients at much diminished values, and that the plan would not remedy this private loss. Many of the current owners were said to be well-to-do speculators who would receive an unearned gain on instruments of public debt which they had accumulated in anticipation of Hamilton's recommendation. But, like many a public policy, this one served a desirable goal at the cost of something less than perfect justice.

Hamilton's third report to the Congress recommended, as almost everybody expected, a federal mint to turn out coins for the national government. Congress acted promptly and favorably; the mint was established in Philadelphia on April 2, 1792. The law decreed a bimetallic standard—15 ounces of silver to 1 ounce of gold (which was about their relationship in the commercial bullion market at the time). There were to be silver coins for the dollar— of the same weight as the Spanish dollar—and for subsidiary currency; gold was to be used for coins of $10, $5, and $2.50. We need not here discuss the monetary difficulties which subsequently arose because of an adverse balance of foreign trade, hoarding, and the fluctuating ratio of the prices of gold and silver. They were annoying, but not of major importance to the nation's growing economy.

Hamilton and Manufacture

The most far-seeing feature of Hamilton's planning for the economic future was his "Report on the Subject of Manufactures," sent to Congress in 1791. The industrial revolution was spreading rapidly in England; one of the causes of the American Revolution consisted of obstacles placed in the way of factory production in the colonies. The traditional practice was for the colonies to export to the mother country food crops and raw materials in return for manufactured goods. Now that independence had been won, the planners of the nation's economy naturally wished to encourage manufacture at home.

Hamilton marshaled arguments and recommended measures to facilitate this aim. Handicrafts existed, but, as Adam Smith had pointed out, division of labor, such as accompanied factory production, greatly enlarged output per worker. Industrial employment would increase the labor force. It would afford more opportunity to differing talents. The growth of an industrial population would enlarge domestic demand for farm products and would encourage immigration of skilled workers. The less skilled jobs could offer employment to women outside the home. And, of course, manufacture would provide outlets for investment of capital earnings.

To encourage manufacture, the government could offer bounties (which now we should call subsidies) and enact protective tariffs on imports—a policy Adam Smith disliked. Construction of highways and canals could widen markets for the products of factories, as such construction had done in England.

The description of the advantages of developing manufacture in this report in 1791 resembles in many ways the thinking of "underdeveloped" nations today. And the report offers a curious parallel (in the climate of capitalistic enterprise) to the later effort of the Soviet Union to develop the resources of a great nation. Both systems require foresight, appropriate governmental measures, and adequate incentives.

Land Planning: Jefferson's Contributions

For nearly two hundred and fifty years after the first white settlers came to the Atlantic coast of North America, land was more abundant than labor. The grants made by the British government to American colonies or favored individuals consisted of land. The land was of little use without labor to cultivate it; consequently there was competition among the owners of landed estates for the services of able-bodied farm workers. Scarcity of labor led to slavery in the South and indentured labor elsewhere. Most of the free workers, in turn, wished to buy farms—usually of "family" size.

Democratic forces during the American Revolution destroyed the remnants of a feudal land system (except in New York State) by confiscating the estates owned by proprietors who remained loyal to the British crown. Legislation by the states prevented the compulsory preservation of great landed estates, by ending primogeniture and entail, the British laws which required that the whole of a landed estate be bequeathed to the oldest son, and that even he could not sell it.

Thomas Jefferson, the chief Revolutionary supporter of democratic government, believed that it could be safeguarded largely through widespread ownership of small farms. He was also impressed by the economic doctrine of the French Physiocrats, prominent before the French Revolution, that the ultimate source of wealth was the land—including the minerals under it—and that the best economic policy was that of laissez faire in production and distribution. His contribution to the planning of the nation's economy consisted largely of promoting ownership of family farms in the still unsettled regions. He also advocated public education which would enable the children of settlers to be intelligent citizens.

At the beginning of the Revolutionary War, the colonies did not own territory west of the Alleghenies. But in the peace treaty Britain ceded the land between the Ohio River, the Great Lakes, and the Mississippi River, still largely unsettled. The Eastern states, which had claimed unsettled Western lands lying in their respective latitudes, ceded their claims to the federal government.

Here was the first great opportunity to serve Jefferson's policy. Even before the adoption of the Constitution, the Congress of the Confederation adopted farsighted ordinances for the future of this Northwest Territory. The Ordinance of 1785 decreed the manner of laying out new townships which has governed the opening of new lands ever since—by quadrangles six miles square, each divided into thirty-six sections of one square mile. One section was the unit of land offered for sale by the government. The minimum price acceptable in public auctions was fixed at $640 per section (equivalent to $1.00 per acre). Section 16 had to be reserved for the town government as a subsidy for the public school.

At a later date most state governments also reserved for this purpose another section, usually number 36.

The Ordinance of 1787 added other important and farsighted policies, then applied only to the Northwest Territory. Slavery and involuntary servitude were forever to be prohibited. The region was to be divided into new territories, not less than three in number or more than five. Federal governors were to be appointed by Congress, one for each territory. As soon as the number of male citizens in any territory numbered five thousand, they were to elect a territorial legislature. When the population reached sixty thousand, the territory could become a state, which must be admitted to the Union with full equality. In this way the states of Ohio, Indiana, Illinois, Michigan, and Wisconsin were created. Except for the prohibition of slavery, which became a ferociously debated issue as regarded several of the new states, the precedent established by the Ordinance of 1787 was followed thereafter as other regions to the west were acquired by the Union and opened to settlement. Automatic admission to the Union as a state, when population grew sufficiently, stood the test of time and held in check any tendency for the nation to become an imperial power in the sense of ruling colonies without equal democratic rights.

In an effort to make it easier for pioneers to obtain land, Congress subsequently reduced the price per acre and permitted installment payment. Several other concessions were made, until in 1862 the Homestead Act permitted any head of a family, twenty-one years old or more, to become the owner of 160 acres of the public domain without any payment, if he lived on it for five consecutive years. No more than 160 acres of land was to be sold to one buyer. That restriction was intended to prevent speculators from obtaining large parcels at the lawful price and selling it later to settlers at higher prices. Speculators found ways of avoiding the intent of the provision. Speculating in land had long been a get-rich-quick device, and, like any rampant speculation financed by bank loans, it has led on occasion to monetary crises. Nevertheless, the plan to populate public lands by selling them to pioneers, who could make a living largely by farming, did achieve its purpose.

When President Jefferson bought from Napoleon the Louisiana

Purchase in 1803, he almost doubled the area of the nation. This act led to planning for the best use of land, which later became a standard policy. The federal government immediately sent an expedition under Meriwether Lewis and William Clark to discover the nature and resources of the newly acquired territory. This was the beginning of a long series of measures by the government to plan the best uses of the great West—including the survey of routes for transcontinental railways, geological surveys, the Reclamation Bureau with its projects for irrigation and other uses of water power, and the establishment of national parks and forests.

Planning Transportation

In the meantime, transportation in the Eastern states demanded planning. When the colonies were all on the Atlantic seaboard, ships and smaller craft plying the coastal waters and navigable rivers carried the freight and most of the passengers. As the nation spread to the west, however, main roads (turnpikes) and canals became necessary. President Jefferson, in his message to Congress on the state of the nation in 1806, declared that customs duties would soon yield a treasury surplus, which should be used for education and transportation facilities. Senator John Quincy Adams in 1807 introduced a resolution that the Secretary of the Treasury be directed to draw up a general plan for internal transportation; the Senate so voted, 22 to 3. Albert Gallatin, the incumbent Secretary, sent his report on the subject to the Senate on April 4, 1808. He argued for a general plan with two main objectives: to connect the states on a north-south axis, and to provide for transport between the seaboard and the West. No single project, he argued, could fulfill its objective well without a complete system.

The Gallatin plan was ingenious and logical. On the north-south waterway, tidewater routes already existed between Massachusetts and Georgia, interrupted by four necks of land: Cape Cod, that part of New Jersey between the Raritan and Delaware Rivers, the peninsula between the Delaware River and Chesapeake Bay, and the marshes between the Chesapeake and Albemarle Sound.

Canals totaling less than a hundred miles in length would cut through all of them. He also recommended a turnpike from Maine to Georgia, connecting all the major ports. For the east-west routes, the head of navigation of each of the main rivers running east to the Atlantic could be connected by turnpikes with the head of navigation of interior rivers running westerly to the Mississippi. These pairs of rivers were the Susquehanna and the Allegheny (which joins the Ohio), the Potomac and the Monongahela, the James and the Kanawha, the Santee or the Savannah and the Tennessee. In addition, the Hudson River could be connected by canals with Lake Ontario or Lake Erie and with Lake Champlain. The western part of the system could be joined by turnpikes with Detroit, St. Louis, and New Orleans.

Secretary Gallatin estimated that appropriations totaling $16.6 million would do the job, and allowed an extra $3.4 million for public works in the states that would not be directly benefited. Thus an annual appropriation of $2 million for ten years, which he thought would be well within the means of the federal government, would suffice.

The plan was interrupted by a sharp decline in tax receipts caused by the embargo against France and Britain, which were interfering with American shipping in their war with each other. The War of 1812 followed. Political controversies about the constitutionality of this use for federal funds, and rivalry among the states, created additional obstacles. Yet much of the plan was, in the long run, executed. New York built the Erie Canal and the canal which connected the Hudson to Lake Champlain. Other states rushed to dig canals and construct turnpikes. After the arrival of the motor car in the twentieth century, the federal government supplied a through highway from Maine to Georgia. And the government eventually brought about the inland coastal waterway, including a canal through Cape Cod. Albert Gallatin's imaginative plan of 1808 was carried out more than a century after he proposed it—although by that time many of the interior canals had been abandoned because of competition from railroads and motor trucks. Federal subsidies for interstate motor-vehicle highways have played a large role in the twentieth century.

The Railroad Era

As soon as a practicable steam locomotive was invented, railroad-building began, and it soon occupied a major place in the economic growth of the young nation. In 1830 there were 32 miles of railroad in the United States; by 1860 there were about 30,000. After the Civil War transcontinental lines were built. Unfortunately, railroad-building was a project in which there was little or no nationwide planning. Although a few states built and owned railways, most of these were constructed and operated by private companies in a scramble for profit. The new lines usually received subsidies from regions and businessmen who feared competition by other regions. The United States Government granted large tracts of public land to railroad companies formed to connect the Middle West with the Pacific. Political corruption and frauds on the part of railroad financiers caused numerous scandals. The inventors, civil engineers, manufacturers of rails and equipment, and operating employees for the most part did their jobs well; the promoters and top managements usually put private gain ahead of the public interest. The nation eventually received the rapid transportation necessary for its development, but the private enterprises involved often cheated the small investors and the customers. Before the age of motor vehicles and aircraft, rail companies encountered little competition from outside the industry; competing railroads, where they existed, often found it easy and profitable to agree on their charges rather than to engage in "rate wars."

At length, enraged shippers demanded regulation of the railroads, first by state governments, the legislators of which were sometimes bribed by the companies, and later by the federal government. The railroad magnates attempted to prevent regulation by appeal to the courts on the ground that governmental supervision was unconstitutional, and eventually lost their case. An Interstate Commerce Commission, created by Congress in 1887, attempted to exercise control over the railroads, but often found itself hampered by litigation. The limited power of the commission gave it no scope to take the initiative in planning. There was a long series of public controversies about railroad services and charges.

The Age of the Robber Barons

As nation-states in Europe began to emerge from medieval feudalism, they built kings' highways to encourage commerce. But some of the feudal lords were strong enough to dominate the highways from their castles, and they levied tribute on the passing merchants or robbed them of everything they owned. In the United States after the Civil War there were robber barons of business who gained or lost enormous fortunes by levying tribute sometimes on the railroads, sometimes on smaller businesses, sometimes on the government or the public at large. An early occasion for this large-scale brigandage was the construction of the first railroad to the Pacific Coast.

During the Civil War, Congress gave a federal charter to the Union Pacific Railroad Company and subsidized it by large grants of public land—not merely enough for the right-of-way, but also twenty square miles of land for every mile of track. The land would have a substantial value after trains began to operate, and meanwhile it could be used as security for bond issues to finance the construction of the railroad.

While construction proceeded with the help of this generous federal subsidy, the officers and directors of the railroad devised an additional scheme to channel money into their own pockets. They acquired ownership of a Pennsylvania corporation called Crédit Mobilier, which submitted bids for the construction work. As officials of the railroad, the owners of Crédit Mobilier accepted the bids which they themselves had made; no competitor had a chance. Thus, they made profits for themselves estimated by a subsequent investigation as 200 per cent above the actual cost of construction. The profits were somewhat diminished, however, by the large bribes they admittedly paid to members of Congress, including both Republicans and Democrats.

Another method used by the robber barons to defraud railroads and other corporations which they controlled was simply to float bond issues for amounts vastly greater than were required. If a railroad, for example, planned new construction costing $50 million, it might issue bonds for $200 million, even though the entire worth of the railroad corporation, including the new construction, might be less than $100 million. The bonds were sold to American and foreign investors, and the extra millions simply disappeared. In later years the railroad would be impoverished by paying interest on the bonds, and in many cases it would be forced into bankruptcy.

Social Darwinism

Between the Civil War and the First World War there were several sharp recessions—notably in 1873, 1883, and 1907—but in general big business thrived and grew bigger. Contrary to the doctrines of Adam Smith, the organizers of what came to be known as "trusts" aimed to eliminate competition at the cost of small business, farmers, the consuming public, and especially labor, which was compelled to work long hours for low wages. As late as 1920 some workers in the steel industry still had a twelve-hour day and a seven-day week. Like the Mercantilists of old, the late-nineteenth-century manufacturers obtained the protection of high tariffs, especially when the Republicans had a majority in both houses of Congress.

In an attempt to dissolve the monopolies, Congress passed the Sherman Antitrust Act in 1890, to prohibit combinations in restraint of trade. The act was difficult to enforce, largely because of the manner in which it was interpreted by conservative federal courts, but also because the monopolists found various devices for circumventing it. Among the devices were trustees empowered to vote a majority of the stock (hence the name "trusts"), "holding companies" with a controlling interest in several manufacturing companies that had once been competitors, and "interlocking directorates" which allowed one group of men to act as directors in many corporations. The Clayton Act of 1914 was designed to end some of these practices, but again the act was not effectively enforced when government officials and judges were conservatives.

Eventually the monopolists became so feared by labor, consumers, farmers, small businessmen, and middle-class reformers that a movement of protest gained wide attention. Big business was assailed in influential books, including Henry Demarest Lloyd's *Wealth against Commonwealth*, Ida M. Tarbell's *History of the Standard Oil Company*, and Lincoln Steffens' *The Shame of the Cities*. Magazines prospered by revealing the sins of the rich. Over a period of more than thirty years the agitation assumed a political form. Populism, which was primarily a movement of poverty-stricken farmers, declined after 1900, but reformers were still winning elections in various states, and in 1912 they formed the basis of a third party, the Progressives.

Against this attack from the left, the conservatives mustered a good deal of academic support. One of their chief arguments was based on the work of Herbert Spencer, the leading British philosopher of the time. Spencer and his disciples had applied Charles Darwin's concept of "the survival of the fittest" to human society, arguing that the big businessmen, the financiers, and other types of successful executives had earned their victories, were fittest to survive, and should be honored as the best guarantees of a brighter future for mankind. "Social Darwinism" was the name applied to this type of thinking.

In the long run, however, the financial lords who ruled the nation during the decades after the Civil War met with a stunning defeat. They had ignored the economic prescriptions of Adam Smith's *The Wealth of Nations* by substituting monopoly for competition. It was a planless monopoly, however, and the financial lords had prevented almost any sort of planning by government for half a century.

CHAPTER 3

We Planned in War (1917-1919)

Social Darwinism was out of fashion in the 1920s, but in those later days conservatives found another line of defense. To proposals that economic life be organized for collective purposes, it was customary for them to answer that the task was beyond human capacity or that, even if it could be done, it was something alien to the peculiar talents and values of America. The objectors forgot that Americans, before the Russian revolution, using their native wit and their domestic resources, once did a remarkable job of planning. Many of those who advocated a planned society in later years had been doing so, in one way or another, ever since the experiences of 1917-1918, and mainly as a result of the possibilities which those experiences suggested for better performance in times of peace.

That used to be a dangerous statement for anyone who believed in planning. To listeners with vivid memories of what happened during World War I, it suggested that the planner wanted such things as heatless Mondays, sugarless coffee, dollar-a-year men, useless wooden ships, Hog Island confusion, an airplane program that produced no airplanes, an artillery program that did not deliver a single gun in France, railroads "undermaintained" while accumulating a huge deficit, big profits for meat-packers, inflated wages, farmers held down to a minimum price for wheat while suffering from a broken promise about the price of pork, and industries accumulating swollen surpluses.

There is no possibility of denying the fumbling, the mistakes, the occasional dishonesties, the annoyances accompanying our industrial mobilization for the First World War. But we cannot understand that experience without recognizing a number of smaller facts and a few big ones. The smaller facts have to do with general misconceptions of what actually occurred. There is no space here to correct these misconceptions with complete citations of chapter and verse, but there is reasonable assurance in the figures that the following assertions are correct.

Profits. Aggregate profits of American industry, though large, were smaller after we went into the war and established controls —in 1917 and particularly in 1918—than they had been in 1916.

Wages. While money wages were increased all round, and the lower wage rates were increased more than the cost of living, so that standards of living rose for the poorer classes of the population, there was little or no average gain in the real wages paid for normal working hours during the war period. Railroad men and other higher wage groups had smaller increases in wage rates than the rise in the cost of living. Labor's chief benefit was from full employment.

Agriculture. While farmers may not have profited so much as owners of industry, they were better off than for many years before or afterward.

Railroads. The railroads had to be taken over by the government—for temporary control—because they had practically broken down under the operating strain. Unified management proved so much more efficient than competition that the tangle was quickly untied and freight kept moving. The deficits which the railroads accumulated during government control were due, not at all to inefficient operation, but chiefly to the fact that it was thought wise, in the interest of the war, not to raise rates as fast as the prices of coal, materials, and equipment were rising. If the railroads had later been as efficiently operated by competing private managements as they were—by railroad men themselves—under unified government control, they would probably have given us better service at a lower cost.

Shipping. In spite of the blunders of shipbuilding and ship control, we were able to neutralize the submarine campaign, transport a large army to France, and supply it, besides sending abroad the materials required by the Allies.

The larger facts are the really striking ones. We took about 10 million men—or one-quarter of our gainfully occupied population —out of the production of goods and services useful in the ordinary life of peace. Some of these men were in the Army, where they were engaged either in the destruction of life and property or in being trained for that destruction. The rest were occupied in equipping those men with the complicated and costly instruments of destruction, and all the other special material which they needed. Ten million of our ordinary productive forces not only had to be fed, clothed, and housed as in peace, but themselves were engaged, directly or indirectly, in active destruction. This immense dislocation was achieved within a few months.

The lesson of this experience cannot be escaped. By a deliberate collective effort, a tremendous expansion of our production was possible. By a deliberate effort, an amazing transfer of industrial energy from certain types of production to other types could be made in a short time. If that military and industrial army had been mobilized, not to kill, burn, and shatter, but to substitute garden cities for slums, to prevent pollution of air and water, to carry out flood control, to increase the necessities of life available for those in the lower income groups, we could have achieved in a short time a large number of really desirable objectives. It is nonsense to say that there is any physical impossibility of doing for peace purposes the sort of thing we actually have done for war purposes. There may be obstructions in our institutions, habits, and desires, but not in our equipment, skill, and intelligence. This is not to say, of course, that we could do the peacetime job in precisely the same way.

Someone may still be objecting that in reality the burden of the First World War was placed on the future, that later we suffered as a result of the extravagances which then were incurred. It is customary to compare a nation at war with an individual living beyond his income, who must subsequently scrimp to pay for his folly. The analogy is not wholly sound. It arises from the confusion of money matters with the physical aspects of our economy. It is true that money was borrowed by the nations at war, and that this money subsequently was expected to be repaid to the lenders, with interest. But the generation which fought the war produced every physical thing which was used by that generation. It did not, in 1917, borrow a cabbage or a tractor or a loaf of bread which did not then exist and had to be produced by a later generation. The full cost of the war, in a real and physical sense, was met while it was being fought. The only true exceptions to this statement must be made in physical terms—as when cattle were killed off faster than they were bred, or machinery was allowed to wear out without being repaired or replaced. So far as the borrowing and repayment of money is concerned, it is not truly a transaction between one generation and the next, but a device which transfers income from one part of the population to another in each generation. When the United States Government borrowed to pay the costs of the war, it was taking money from lenders to avoid taking more currently from taxpayers. The result was that subsequently it had to take more from taxpayers to repay lenders. This is essentially a redistribution of the available financial income existing at each time.

The economic consequences of the First World War and of the peace settlement were, to be sure, both tremendous. All sorts of dislocation of prices, of trade channels, of debts, of income distribution, followed. But the later sufferings were caused largely not because the war consumed physical goods, but because we did not make the readjustment from war to peace as intelligently as we made the adjustment from peace to war. We did not learn how to use our stores of material, equipment, and energy as efficiently for peace purposes as we did for war purposes. We organized to change over from peace production to war production, but we did not organize to change back; instead we abandoned organization as far as we could.

Financing the War

The temporary planned economy during World War I grew out of practical necessity. Its basic concern was to allocate the output and resources of the nation in such a way that, in addition to supplying ordinary domestic necessities, it could export unusually large quantities of food, other natural resources, and munitions of war, build rapidly new fleets of merchant ships and naval vessels, and gather and equip armed services of some 4 million men. Of the civilian labor force of 36 million, about 9 million were working in war industries when hostilities ended.

Governments were the main buyers. The United States was of course the largest buyer of all, but in allocating resources it had to supply the needs of its allies and associates. Two major essentials had to be provided as the basis of the task. First, there must be an ample flow of money to the governmental agencies which did the buying. Second—and much more difficult—the many and various purchases must be coordinated to the end that needs might be met in the most efficient way and in the order of importance.

Let us begin by examining the sources and amount of the money mobilized to pay the bills.

Between January 1915, five months after the war in Europe began, and April 6, 1917, when the United States entered it, the European belligerents rapidly expanded their purchases in this country. In order to do so, the Allies borrowed dollars by selling new bond issues in the United States, and they also sold already existing securities representing former investments made in this country by their citizens. The amount of money so mobilized while the United States was still a neutral was at least $5 billion. At this time the Gross National Product in the United States averaged about $40 billion annually. During 1915, 1916, and 1917 the Allies bought in the United States nearly seven times as much wheat as in the three years before the war, twice as much wheat flour, and nearly two and one-half times as much meat. Their purchases of minerals and munitions greatly stimulated American mining and manufacturing industries.

When the United States entered the war, its national partners had found difficulty in floating new bond issues for public sale and had disposed of most of the investments formerly made in this country by their citizens. Therefore the United States Government financed their American purchases. Before the war there had been no intergovernmental debts, but during the war the Allies borrowed $9.591 billion, spent for American-produced food and munitions.

Added to this stimulus to the United States economy were the orders by the American war agencies. Later the United States Treasury Department calculated the total war spending in this country. The United States Government spent, net, for war between April 6, 1917, and June 30, 1920, about $22.25 billion. Adding the amount spent here by other nations brought the total to slightly less than $31.5 billion. According to an estimate by the National Bureau of Economic Research, war spending ranged from one-sixth to one-fourth of the annual national income in 1917 and 1918.

If the government had relied entirely on tax revenues, the taxes would have decreased the incomes of individuals and business concerns as much as the governmental spending for war increased them. Total demand, in spite of the enormous war spending, would have been the same as in peace. But in fact, of the total governmental expenditure only $10.7 billion was derived from taxes in excess of the estimated normal budget, and about $23 billion was obtained by sale of United States bond issues. The purchasers of these bonds could, and usually did, borrow from banks in order to buy them, so that about one-third of the government spending was supplied by bank-created credit. Total purchasing power, including governmental and private buyers, was markedly increased. This situation led to three desirable major guides of economic planning in wartime, as follows:

1. Production of military and civilian necessities should be encouraged, while unnecessary production should be restricted.
2. Order and efficiency should be observed in the purchases of governmental agencies.
3. In many cases price-control would be desirable, especially in those sectors of the economy where demand greatly exceeded supply.

The Results of Planning

The effectiveness of the war planning can be measured both by large totals of production and by changes within them. Before the United States entered the war in April 1917, the military component of the Gross National Product, measured in 1914 prices, had increased over 1914 by only $100 million, while the nonwar component grew more than fifty times as much—$5.1 billion. But between the first quarter of 1917 (after which the nation was a belligerent and adopted planning) and the fourth quarter of 1918, when the war ended, the war component of the GNP increased by $11.2 billion, while the nonwar component *decreased* by $13 billion.

Under governmental control, the number of new railroad locomotives increased from 4075 in 1916 to 6475 in 1918. Gross tonnage of new ships grew from 325,000 in 1916 to 1,301,000 in 1918. Output of aluminum was enlarged from 110.2 million pounds in 1916 to 132.3 million pounds in 1918. Steel output had already reached its maximum by 1917. But output of consumer goods, for the most part, declined; for example, the manufacture of passenger automobiles was drastically reduced. About the only exception consisted of cigarettes, the smoking of which became a national habit. The number of cigarettes manufactured leaped from 17,944 million in 1914 to 47,528 million in 1918.

The large increase in governmental demand, combined with a fully employed labor force, both sectors spending money which in large part was created by bank credit, exerted a powerful force to raise prices. War planning did relatively little to restrain the advance. By 1918 the index of wholesale prices of all commodities had risen 98.4 per cent above the 1913 level—the last year of peace. No legislation enforced retail price-control or a rationing system, such as were later employed in World War II. The price-regulation adopted was applied mainly to raw materials the prices of which rose 88.9 per cent between 1913 and 1918, or about 10 per cent less than wholesale prices. Retail prices, which as a rule rise more slowly than wholesale, were, in 1918, 50 per cent above the level of 1914. Labor benefited by wage adjustments intended to increase rates of pay as much as the rise in cost of living, but these lagged behind the upward trend of retail prices. Labor's chief gains, as has been said, were the result of full employment. J. M. Clark later estimated that of the $31 billion cost of the war, $18 billion was derived from decreased civilian consumption after 1915.

Business concerns of course received extraordinarily large profits. But, in addition to ordinary corporation income taxes, the government imposed excess-profits taxes applied to earnings greater than those received before the war. In the fiscal year ended June 30, 1918, excess-profits taxes yielded $2227 million in addition to the ordinary corporation income tax. Personal income taxes in the same year yielded $663 million. By these means government received for war expenditure much of the private gain arising from failure to limit prices, and thereby diminished the necessity to borrow. The chief beneficiaries of war prosperity bought a major share of the governmental war-bond issues. About 30 per cent of the bonds were sold to individuals with incomes of $2000 or less, who in this way contributed $7 billion. Those with incomes above $2000 bought about $10 billion of bonds, and nearly $6 billion were bought by corporations. In addition, business concerns used part of their profits for direct investment in productive machinery for war work. Much of this equipment could be used for civilian production after peace came. But J. M. Clark concludes that during the war the owners of income-yielding property, after paying income taxes and purchasing bonds, had a diminished amount to spend for personal goods and services.

Meanwhile the nation succeeded in supporting its allies with food and munitions, limited the German submarine campaign, raised and equipped a large army, and transported to Europe enough troops to make victory possible. To be sure, most of the emergency fleet was not completed until after the victory; but improved management of existing shipping supplied the necessary transports.

The Planning Agencies

Before the United States entered the war, the immense pressure of demand from the Allied belligerents and from the United States Government influenced both businessmen and public officials to attempt to create some order in the nation's economy.

As early as December 7, 1915, President Wilson's message to Congress had recommended building "a navy second to none." The Congress promptly accepted the project. Shipbuilding was already booming. A civilian Naval Consulting Board, picked from scientific societies, had recognized that the Army as well as the Navy might need help, and in August 1915 created a Committee for Industrial Preparedness, financed by private contributions, which compiled an inventory of manufacturing plants capable of making munitions.

In June 1916 Congress passed a National Defense Act, which contained clauses giving the President power to order war material, to commandeer manufacturing plants, and to appoint an industrial mobilization board. Naturally the legislators expected the President to delegate these powers. On August 29 of the same year a Military Appropriations Act created a Council of National Defense composed of cabinet officers, which in turn delegated most of its work to an Advisory Commission of leading citizens.

Boards and committees, with their subordinate agencies, proliferated. As "preparedness" approached the declaration of war in April 1917, Washington was full of "dollar-a-year men," for the most part business executives who contributed their services to the governmental mobilization of economic resources.

Confusion reigned, as the various bureaus in the War and Navy Departments, the Emergency Fleet Corporation (a subsidiary of the Shipping Board), and other governmental agencies tried to estimate their several needs and find the sources to supply them. As yet there were no price-controls, even of raw materials. A General Munitions Board unsuccessfully tried to coordinate the ensuing scramble. On July 8, 1917—after the nation had been at war more than three months—the Council of National Defense established a War Industries Board, consisting of five civilians and one representative each of the Army and the Navy. It prepared for necessary fact-finding but had no executive power. The first chairman, unable to end the confusion, resigned, and the second, Daniel Willard, the socially minded and successful president of the Baltimore and Ohio Railroad, soon followed his example. The forces of competition, not only among business firms but among governmental agencies, could not be successfully coordinated to meet the national need at a time when the total of demand seemed greatly to exceed the supply. At least they could not be governed by an agency which could not legally enforce its decisions.

The War Industries Board

In the spring of 1918 President Wilson reorganized the War Industries Board and commanded it to coordinate war industries. As chairman he appointed Bernard Baruch, who would exercise final authority over every activity of the board except price-fixing. That was to be the duty of a committee of the board responsible directly to the President, who had received broad war powers from Congress. A letter from the President to Baruch outlined his responsibility (March 4, 1918). The board was instructed:

> to create new facilities and find new sources of supply;
> to conserve resources by economies in their use;
> to determine priorities in production and delivery;
> to allocate among the various purchasing agencies the available supplies whenever a shortage appeared;
> to be purchasing agent for the Allies.

Other existing governmental administrations, such as those having to do with food, fuel, shipping, the railways, and foreign trade, had representatives on the War Industries Board Committee in charge of priorities.

The board itself never made any purchases or sales—except for the European Allies. But it did become a powerful alternative for "free, competitive markets" in the distribution of goods. The board substituted national needs for the customary sale to the highest bidder.

In carrying out its function, it naturally attempted to keep prices down, since the purchases of war goods were allocated according to need rather than by market prices. The price-control was applied first, and mainly, to raw materials and intermediate products such as steel. Toward the end of the war, economists on the board's staff were at work on a more fully developed price-control which would extend the system through to purchases by consumers, but their task was not completed when peace came.

The Food Administration

The Food Administration, unlike the War Industries Board, was created by Congressional statute—the Lever Bill, which became law on August 10, 1917. On the same day the President appointed as administrator Herbert Hoover, who had acquired a favorable reputation by his work on Belgian relief. His task, in broad terms, was much the same as that of the War Industries Board. It was his duty to see that both the Allies and the United States obtained enough food, at prices within their means. The law gave him three specified powers: first, to make voluntary agreements with farmers or food industries; second, to license business concerns and prescribe regulations for the licensed firms; and, third, to buy and sell foodstuffs. All these powers he shrewdly exercised.

To deal with the grain supply and its prices he used the bargaining power of a governmentally owned United States Grain Corporation, which acted as buying agent for food ordered by the Allies as well as for grain for domestic consumption. The Grain Corporation guaranteed that farmers would receive a minimum price on wheat and other staples, no matter how much they might produce, and maintained that price by buying and selling in the market instead of relying on the ordinary competitive bidding of private business. The price was probably not so high as private market trading might have brought, but it was high enough to yield an assured profit to the growers for a whole crop-year at a time, and so to encourage an increase in the crops. The Grain Corporation also rationalized the storing and transport of the crops, by agreements with grain elevators, railroads, and other means of storage and transportation.

To prevent runaway increases in the selling prices of food-processing plants, the Food Administration made several hundred agreements with the companies concerned, specifying output, prices, and profits. Since the administration had the legal right to set up a licensing system in any food industry, it had the power to see that the agreements were carried out. A frequent device was to allow fixed margins between cost of materials and selling prices.

Another ingenious plan was the Sugar Equalization Board. The costs of production of sugar cane and beets varied among the several growing regions in the United States, Cuba, Hawaii, Puerto Rico, and the Philippines. In a free, competitive market, the cost of the whole crop would tend to be the price of sugar in the growing region with the highest costs, at a time when the demand for sugar was greater than the supply. The Sugar Equalization Board arranged with each growing region to buy its total output at a price which would stimulate production in that region. The American refiners agreed to buy sugar only from the Equalization Board, and to pay for it 7.28 cents a pound, which was the weighted average of the prices assigned to the several growing regions.

These devices did yield increased profits to most of the food-processing industries, as well as to farmers. The greater part of the profits, however, probably represented larger volume of output rather than price increases. When the Food Administration began its operations in August 1917, wholesale food prices had already risen 80 per cent above 1913. After that, food prices showed little increase, in comparison with other costs. The Food Administration did reduce the margin between wholesale and retail food prices from 47 per cent in 1915 and 1916 to less than 40 per cent at the end of 1917 and thereafter.

Labor Standards

One of the most vital scarcities of the war economy consisted of civilian labor. Demand for processed or manufactured goods was immense. Meanwhile the number of wage-earners was reduced by enlistment in the armed forces. Involuntary unemployment virtually disappeared. There was a need not only to prevent work stoppages caused by strikes or lockouts, but to use as efficiently as possible the manpower available.

With the cooperation of the American Federation of Labor, and the authorities of the numerous governmental purchasing agencies, both aims were well served. Collective bargaining was permitted; unions were recognized. Disagreements were resolved, when necessary, by arbitration. The standard working day of eight hours—a goal long fought for by the labor movement—was established in most industries, with extra pay for overtime. The national government created a nationwide network of employment agencies, which war contractors were compelled to use in augmenting their work forces. Women—many of whom now joined the labor force—received wages equal to those of men in the same jobs.

Transportation Industries: Ships and Railroads

The British merchant marine had long been the chief ocean carrier when the war began. United States shipping companies then had only about one-fourth as much tonnage as the British, and much of this was used for coastal freight. During the war, Britain had to curtail ship building to about one-third of peacetime output, because of more immediate war demands for armament and manpower. In addition, by the time the United States declared war, German submarines had sunk nearly one-fourth of British merchant shipping.

American shipbuilders had greatly enlarged their output to satisfy the extraordinary demand. But their total tonnage of new ships finished in 1916 was only about one-fourteenth of the war losses of shipping. Congress in 1916 established a United States Shipping Board to manage the existing merchant fleet, and appropriated $50 million for ship building, to be carried out by an Emergency Fleet Corporation. The first new ship of its ambitious program was not delivered until December 1918, when President Wilson went to Europe to arrange the terms of peace. Meanwhile the Shipping Board took charge of all the existing ships, including not only the United States vessels, but 97 interned German ships, which needed repairs, and 87 Dutch ships, which had been laid up by their owners because of the submarine danger. British shipping joined the pool. This monopoly greatly increased cargoes per ship; and the time used to unload and take on cargoes was on the average cut in half. Thus, by carefully planned operations, the board managed to transport the necessary freight and the United States armies, with their equipment. This achievement was made possible by the Shipping Board's Division of Planning and Statistics, under the direction of Edwin F. Gay, Dean of the Harvard Graduate School of Business Administration. It was an example of the superiority of well-planned monopoly acting in the public interest over competitive private enterprise.

A similar plan enabled the railroads to serve the national interest. Many of the railroad companies were carrying excessive mortgages and loans, had little credit in the money markets, and were underequipped. Competition led to unnecessary cross-hauls, unnecessary terminal facilities, and the underuse of freight cars, which, although they often traveled on many railroads to reach their destinations, had to be routed back empty to the owning company. This waste was particularly large because an unusually large part of the freight was shipped from the interior of the nation to the Atlantic Coast, so that even a railroad which had terminals at both ends apparently had to return many of its cars empty on the return journey. In 1915 there was a net surplus of freight cars; a shortage appeared in early 1916. In 1917 the railroads had a shortage ranging usually between 100,000 and 150,000. The roads were burdened with the largest traffic in their history. Obviously what the industry required was abandonment of competition and a pooling of services.

In 1917 the railroad companies themselves attempted unification by a voluntary Railroad War Board, but it was hampered in the attempt to rationalize freight movements because it had no means by which to compensate any road when traffic was diverted from its lines. It became obvious that if the roads were to do the job, they must, for the time being, be unified under a national agency. To do this job the government created the Railroad Administration. By contract it guaranteed to each railroad a standard return based on its earnings in the years 1914-1917. Skilled railroad men took charge as employees of the national Railroad Administration. Thus it was possible to direct traffic by the shortest routes, to use cars and locomotives wherever the need was greatest, to enforce common use of terminals, to coordinate railroad deliveries with ocean shipping, and to give priorities to shipments that could be removed by the consignees soon after arrival.

The Railroad Administration in 1918 transported about 10 million ton-miles more than the separate companies had handled in 1917. It increased the average carload and the average trainload. The net shortage of freight cars disappeared; by the end of the year there was a surplus of 300,000. It financed payment of the standard return, necessary repairs, and new equipment from a revolving fund appropriated by Congress, rather than by allowing railroad rate increases, except one of 25 per cent soon after the administration began its job. The reason for not allowing rates high enough to cover all expenses was that it would be cheaper in the end for the taxpayers to subsidize railroad traffic than to allow rate increases which would raise the prices of most of the goods the railroads carried.

The Nature of the Planning

Unlike the Soviet Union, the United States in its war planning did not substitute state ownership of the means of production for private enterprise. Rather, it gained its success by channeling a large share of market demand through national agencies. As a dominant purchaser, the government could do much to increase the total output of the nation and to adjust it to the most pressing needs. The economy could thus be rationalized and made more efficient. The ultimate source of this economic power was the ability of the government to flood the economic system with purchasing power, through governmental borrowing and taxation of excess profits. Might not this experience contribute to the welfare of the nation when the enemy was no longer a hostile power, but unemployment and depression? Could it not be used to stimulate economic growth? Such questions remained in the minds of many who understood the economic victory of the United States in World War I.

CHAPTER 4

Return to "Normalcy"

Many leaders of thought hoped that, after the war was ended, national economic planning would be retained—though suitably adjusted—to achieve long-desired reforms. Progressives had not forgotten former President Theodore Roosevelt's New Nationalism of the 1912 campaign. In 1904 he had sponsored a Square Deal. Eight years later he proclaimed that he believed not only in fair play under existing rules of the game, but in "having those rules changed so as to work for a more substantial equality of opportunity and of reward for equally good service." This was the program he christened "The New Nationalism." Roosevelt Progressives had been influenced by Herbert Croly's book, *The Promise of American Life*, which argued that a Hamiltonian philosophy of government should be employed for Jeffersonian ends. By this he meant that liberals should make use of a powerful national government to fulfill the American dream of political equality and progress for all citizens.

President Wilson, before the war, had sponsored much-needed reforms. Congress, in his first term of office, had established the Federal Reserve System (described in Chapter 5) as a national control of banking policy. He had also obtained statutes to curb private business monopolies—the Clayton Antitrust Act and the Federal Trade Commission Act. Liberal supporters of Wilsonian policy might readily have joined Roosevelt Progressives in wishing to retain national planning for guiding the economy in peace.

Theodore Roosevelt, however, died of heart trouble shortly after the war was won. After the victory in 1918, President Wilson was absorbed in negotiating the peace terms, in the formation of

the League of Nations, and in attempting to persuade Americans
to join it. He had to deal not only with the isolationists who had
opposed entering the war in the first place, but also with a war-
weary public that wished to forget the conflict. Business executives who had taken part in the war agencies wanted to close their
Washington offices and go home; the returning soldiers wanted to
go back to civilian life. If planning in peace was to be attempted,
it would have to wait for a new administration. Then in 1920 the
Republican Party nominated Warren Gamaliel Harding, a right-
wing Senator who had consistently served the moneyed interests,
and who now declared that he favored a "return to normalcy."
He was elected President.

The Dream of a New Society

Before 1914 there had been a naïve faith in millennialism. Science
and invention were preparing the way for the fulfillment of civilization. New wonders seemed daily to enlarge the powers and satisfactions of mankind. Injustices and confusions existed, but there
was belief that they would shortly be surmounted. The intellectual
leaders of the time directed attention toward the common life, and
prescribed one or another type of remedy for its ills.

The war shocked American liberals by its revelation of the
survival and diabolical power of forces which the late Victorians
had assumed were buried with the old centuries. But at the same
time it intensified the drive for social change. This conflict, so
liberals believed, was the death spasm of a passing order. War and
revolution are twins. A large body of opinion supposed that the
anachronistic forces of destruction were personified by Germany
and would finally be shut into the past with her defeat. Once this
ugly task was completed, something could be done. This nation
could proceed to organize a new civilization, fit for the maturity
of the human race. International peace and justice, leading to disarmament, would be established by a League of Nations. As for
economic organization, one could choose among a number of well-
defined and neatly cohesive schemes of reform or revolution. The
socialists had one program, the syndicalists another, the guild socialists a third, the consumers' cooperatives a fourth. The Cath-

olic intellectuals, opposing the "servile state," offered their program of "distributivism." Almost all sensitive and active minds were engaged in one public cause or another, whether it was feminism and votes for women, the enlargement of the labor movement, the political program of the British Labor Party, the Plumb Plan for railroads in the United States, or nationalization of the mines. People read, and debated about, H. G. Wells, Bernard Shaw, Sidney Webb, G. D. H. Cole, Georges Sorel, or G. K. Chesterton and Hilaire Belloc.

These ideas and efforts were significant in that they provided an outlet for the personality. They attracted people because they appeared to offer genuine values. The tides of the world were flowing, and carried us along. American liberals saw successively the Russian, German, and minor revolutions, the turbid political movements of labor in other nations, and the great strikes in basic industries even in this country, with millions of men fighting for status in coal, steel, railroads. These activities engrossed emotions, they drew people out of themselves, they provided something to do and something to think. There was a faith that the individual was related to society, that what he could do would have some effect upon it, that social forces in turn would confer values upon him. The times were turbulent, dangerous, uncertain, and full of meaning.

The Great Retreat

This belief in millennialism, the new decade, beginning in 1920, ended with a full stop. The first collapse came in international affairs. As the controversy raged over the war settlement, it became clear that all the destructive forces had not been embodied in one nation and one ruling class; that we could not chop off the head of the old tyrant with a single stroke. Imperialism, secret diplomatic intrigue, militarism, the spirit of national aggrandizement, those personal devils which the less cynical had been led to believe were to be defeated with Germany, raised their heads everywhere. The Treaty of Versailles, with its economically and politically unstable provisions, was the result. The League of Na-

tions was erected askew on unsound foundations. Vested interests
were sluggishly determined that nothing really new should come
about—only a shifting of dominance from one set of powers to
another. The interests had used Wilsonian idealism, enlisting the
moral energy which it released in this country and all over the
world, in behalf of their hidden purposes and had finally exposed
it as a dangerous fraud. The younger generations came to believe
that the war had been a death spasm, not so much of the old, the
ugly, and the detestable, as of facile idealism and meaningless
morality. They would take care not to be wasted again in any such
exhausting millennial effort. The more expansive and generous
impulses of mankind were distrusted as traitors to personal integ-
rity. The young chose, for the sake of their souls, to be incred-
ulous and hard-boiled.

The United States, revolting inchoately against the whole liberal mythology of the war, returned to the dogma of isolation.
Americans had been brought up on the belief that their country
embodied a new hope, a civilization different from that of Europe
and superior to it. We had turned aside to engage in a European
struggle and had got nothing out of it—not even the ideals and
the new world for which we had been told we were unselfishly
fighting. The groups which all along had denied those international
ideals gained supremacy. Though it was impossible for the reac-
tionary forces to acknowledge that our participation in the war
had been a mistake, they justified it not as a combat for positive
purposes and a new civilization, but as chastisement of a single
foreign power which had offended and threatened us. That done,
we must withdraw again within our shell. We must repudiate all
collaboration with Europe, all internationalism. We must raise
tariffs on foreign goods, exclude foreign immigrants, embargo foreign ideas. We must collect the war debts in full. Americanism
was to be our salvation.

The international retreat gave a signal for retreat on all fronts
within the United States. The only meeting ground of minds was
the conviction that terrific mistakes had been made, that the world
was in a bad way. But this conviction led not to a unified and or-

derly advance but to a rout of scattered forces, each of which
sought protection in setting up distinctions as a basis for hatred,
fear, and denunciation. Primitive and exclusive dogmas were ex-
humed as means of salvation.

In politics we had the "return to normalcy," which consisted
in electing as President one of the shallowest, cheapest, and most
boss-ridden politicians in the Senate, whose associates in government were more corrupt than those of any other President since
Grant, and who died on the verge of public disgrace.

In industry we had the drive to scrap every vestige of control
in the interest of the public or the consumer which had been built
up during the war, combined with a determined effort to prevent
the erection of anything better in its place. We had the indiscrim-
inate attack upon all the newer economic and social theories, in
the name of patriotism, by means of denunciation, spying, provo-
cation, blacklists, illegal seizures and searches, deportations, sup-
pressions, and imprisonments. We had the warfare against labor
organization and collective bargaining, carried on under the ban-
ner of "The American Plan," and executed by means of propa-
ganda, corruption, under-cover work, injunctions, hired thugs,
and police forces subservient to employing interests. The acquisi-
tive individualistic businessman was enthroned, without check or
restriction from government, consumer, press, or labor, as the
supposed master of our economic destinies.

This revulsion was far from being a mere scramble of selfish
persons for private gain. It had its own philosophy, ardently invoked and sincerely believed. It was a retreat to American national
fundamentalism—the belief that our all-wise and prophetic group
of "founding fathers" had brought into being a final Constitution
which needed, not to be changed or perfected with the passage of
the decades and the centuries, but to be preserved intact. It was
the belief that the Americans were a chosen people, superior to
all others, who would fulfill their miraculous destiny and prosper
in their land by prosecuting their own concerns in the traditional
individualistic way and by incanting the Bill of Rights (with special emphasis on the right of property).

Postwar Unemployment

When the nation went on a spree of nearly unplanned private enterprise, the first to suffer were soldiers and sailors discharged from the armed forces. Agencies in the Department of War had begun to plan for the transition. Secretary Baker accepted their suggestion of discharging first the men trained for jobs in which vacancies existed, but the Chief of Staff rejected this policy. The War Industries Board tried to plan for placement of the veterans but could not elicit from employers the necessary information. The United States Employment Service placed representatives in every army camp, but Congress soon hampered this effort; it reduced the appropriation for the service by 80 per cent. Many of its staff volunteered to carry on their work without pay, but the number of employment offices was decreased by 260 of the former 750. Some thought that unemployment might be remedied by public works, but Congress would appropriate nothing for the purpose. States and local governments did not respond to an appeal by President Wilson for new construction. The index of building in 1919 was 11 per cent less than the prewar level. Industrial production declined sharply between the third quarter of 1918 and the second quarter of 1919. One estimate placed the unemployed at 3 million, or about 7.5 per cent of the labor force. In many cities men in uniform sold apples on street corners; some became panhandlers.

During the war wage-earners who belonged to unions could maintain standards of working hours and wages by arbitration. But not all wage-earners were organized, and soon after the coming of peace the War Labor Board vanished. Many citizens were startled when in 1919 a newly organized union in the steel industry demanded the six-day week and the eight-hour day; at that time the workers on the blast furnaces were subjected to a seven-day week and a twelve-hour day. Judge Gary, Chairman of United States Steel, not only refused to change this practice, but would not confer with representatives of the union. Coal miners, who had long been unionized, demanded better pay and conditions of work; a federal judge issued an injunction forbidding the strike. Railroad shopmen struck for improvement of wages. There were no federal laws establishing minimum wages and maximum hours, to substitute for the labor administration which had heard and adjusted working standards and wages during the war. "Business as usual" in many cases meant absence of collective bargaining.

Inflation

The unemployment of veterans was of short duration, but unfortunately it was succeeded by an epidemic of price inflation. Prices soared after the armistice. As usual in such a period, speculation for the rise appeared both in capital markets and in transactions of goods. Meanwhile ultimate consumers had to cope with retail prices which rose more rapidly than their incomes. The record is briefly summarized in the following table—which does not show the highest point in either year, since the figures are averages for the twelve months.

PRICE INFLATION 1918-1920

| | Per cent of 1913 level | |
Prices	1918	1920
Wholesale	195.7	227.9
Raw materials	188.9	202.2
Manufactured goods	198.4	239.5
Raw farm products	206.3	212.9
Processed farm products	201.1	241.9
Cost of living	*	205.0

* 177 in 1919

A major influence in bringing about this rapid rise of prices was the issuance in 1919 of a final Victory Loan by the United States, accompanied by a budgetary deficit of more than $4.5 billion. The bonds, as usual, could be used by their purchasers as collateral for loans from the banks. Totals of bank loans and money in circulation expanded as long as the boom lasted. The Federal Reserve Board warned the banks against making loans to be used in speculation and urged the Reserve banks to reduce their discounts, but this had little effect, partly because it was difficult to discover for what purposes the loans were being used.

The government, after the sudden end of such price-controls as had existed during the war, could not stem the price increases.

The many seagoing vessels under construction when the war ended, under the authority of the Emergency Fleet Corporation, were launched and completed after the armistice, in the hope of creating a national Merchant Marine. Even more effectual in sustaining public spending was the financing of orders from the Allies for food stocks, railroad equipment, and other necessities. Also, the authorities in Washington desired to encourage spending by American citizens in order to provide full employment— although, as it eventually turned out, the policy took effect more in raising prices than in expanding output. The automobile industry was an exception; it enlarged production for civilian buying. On the whole, however, the citizens could not greatly increase their purchases, since personal incomes did not keep pace with the soaring prices.

Subsequent analysis indicated that business concerns played a large role in the inflation by speculation in inventories. Expecting higher prices when the finished goods were sold, they borrowed freely to purchase materials and semi-finished or final products. In many cases they placed duplicate orders to be sure of obtaining the goods. During 1919 estimated increase in the value of inventories was $6 billion, almost four times as large as in any year of the ensuing decade except 1923, and almost twice as much as in 1923. About two-thirds of the increase in inventories represented expansion of physical goods; the other one-third was due to rising prices. The inflated inventory values appeared on the books as assets. Meanwhile, there occurred a corresponding expansion of debts to banks, which advanced the necessary credits, often on collateral represented by the inventory stocks.

Deflation

Obviously, the top-heavy economy was overripe for a fall. The collapse occurred in 1920-21, and it was one of the sharpest recessions, especially in drop of prices, that the nation had ever experienced. Wholesale prices fell from an index number of 227.9 in 1920 to 150.6 in 1921 (1913 = 100). Farm products and raw materials declined more than this. Wheat fell from $2.50 a bushel to less than $1.00 in the autumn of 1921; corn, which sold at the farm for $1.88 in 1919, fell to 42 cents in 1921. An estimate of unemployment in 1921 placed it at 4,754,000. About 453,000 farmers lost their farms, in the end. There were more than 100,000 business bankruptcies.

At this time the economic doctrines of John Maynard Keynes had not been constructed, and the effect of the government's budgetary surplus or deficit had not been observed. In retrospect, however, the course of events fits nicely with the Keynes analysis. In the last half of 1918 the federal government spent almost $9 billion in excess of its tax receipts. That pumped money into the economy. In the last quarter of 1919 and the first six months of 1920 the government's tax receipts were $831 million more than it spent. It was thus pumping money out of the private economy, instead of pumping money into it as before. Almost simultaneously, the expansion of bank loans was sharply curbed. Farmers, businessmen, and speculators bitterly opposed this restrictive policy, but under the basic law of the Federal Reserve System the gold reserve had to be not less than 40 per cent of the money supply, and that point was in clear sight. Discount rates were increased; the total of discounts fell from a peak of $2.8 billion in October 1920 to $397 million in August 1922, and federal reserve notes in circulation were diminished by more than $1 billion in 1921.

But the resulting depression, though severe, was of short duration. By the following year the nation had entered a period that would soon be described as the New Era.

The Return of Prosperity

What the New Era meant was the subordination of politics, religion, literature, and the arts to business, and the suppression even of economic movements believed inimical to the supremacy of the businessman (like labor organizations or agricultural factions). There is no question that, during the 1920s, business would be supreme. That does not mean that business itself was organized to control economic life. The nation was not dominated by an industrial government or an economic dictatorship; far from it— economic processes went on in the usual unplanned and competitive anarchy, tempered here and there by groups of monopolistic special privilege. Business controlled politics and the press, but only for the sake of disarming any threat of further control over itself; only in order to maintain the freedom of a hydra-headed private enterprise to do what it pleased, or what it could.

The stimulus was supposed to be competition for profit; the means of advance was business ingenuity making use of science; the result, "prosperity." In prosperity the more alert and deserving would gain riches and would inevitably pull after them the general population; only the defective, the lazy, and the unthrifty would suffer privation, and about these it was unnecessary to worry. Charity would care for them sufficiently to satisfy the conscience of professed religion.

As if to sanction this creed, prosperity came. It was subject to brief and comparatively slight interruptions in 1924 and 1927, but it was swept on apparently by irresistible force. Late in the decade, statistical measures were applied to it, and, being published, were incorporated as the more substantial part of the prosperity myth, which had by this time captured a large popular faith. The purchasing power of the national income per capita of the population grew 22 per cent between 1922 and 1928—and the figure of 1922 had been about the same as that of 1913. The country was, on the average, nearly one-fourth better off than before the war, and the gain had been made in six or seven years. Primary production was growing at the rate of 2½ per cent a year, manufacturing production at the rate of 4 per cent a year, railroad transportation at the rate of 4 per cent. These measurements were not in delusive dollars, which may buy more or less according to what prices are, but in actual physical quantities of goods made and shipped. And when we came to the financial results by which everything else was finally judged in the minds of the dominant groups, the record was even more startling. Profits of all industrial corporations were growing—in the aggregate, and including the laggards as well as the leaders—by no less than 9 per cent a year. At this rate they would double in less than a decade. Dividend payments of industrial and miscellaneous corporations increased nearly 7 per cent a year. And the prices of industrial common stocks had been rising at the astounding rate of 14 per cent a year even by 1927, before the final great bull market started.

Other figures might be recorded, to the extent of volumes, but it is unnecessary for the present purpose to do more than remind ourselves that, however transitory prosperity was, it had substance while it lasted. It was not a mere delusion, a mere manipulation of paper values, a mere point of view. The United States industrial plant actually turned out and distributed a volume of goods larger than ever before known in the world, larger per capita than in any other country, and with a rapidity of growth which was, at the time, almost unprecedented.

No wonder that business was triumphant and that a popular literature and a popular faith were built up about it. Observers came from other nations to discover how we had done it. They wrote their impressions in flattering terms. Our own writers enlarged upon the theories the foreigners advanced. Toward the end of the period a full and rounded myth of prosperity had been furbished out to supply the need for an object of faith.

We had, by and large, been the beneficiaries of good luck; but the result was pictured as the result of conscious policy and control, exercised in behalf of the public welfare. The myth was a rationalization of what had happened.

There was, for instance, the doctrine of the economy of high wages, which assumed that employers, having decided that high wages were necessary in order to supply the workers with sufficient purchasing power to absorb the increasing quantity of goods produced, deliberately paid high rates. They could do so because engineering marvels enabled them to produce continually increasing quantities of goods at continually lower costs.

There was the doctrine of steady improvement in efficiency and scientific method, the benefits of which were rapidly conveyed to the public in the form of reduced prices and improved products,

products widely distributed by means of extremely energetic sales-manship and advertising. Installment credit was enabling every-one to have automobiles, radios, and many other new luxuries, thus furnishing a stimulant to production which was assumed to be permanent.

There was the doctrine of the spreading of ownership and the large profits therefrom throughout the entire population by means of almost universal acquisition of securities, and especially of com-mon stock—a comfortable doctrine which removed any obliga-tion to be troubled by the fact that profits were growing much more rapidly than wages or small salaries. There was the doctrine that business, by merger into larger and larger units, was rationalizing itself for the production of better service and bigger profits. To link the whole together, all fears for the future were banished. We were in a New Era wherein not only would poverty be abolished but everyone would become rich. The symbol of this was an end-less bull market in Wall Street, about which, at the end of the period, the entire national consciousness and will appeared to be gathered with an almost religious enthusiasm.

Not Everyone Was Prosperous

The same objective economic analysis which had verified the cheerful figures also called attention, however, to some deep shad-ows in the picture—shadows which the purveyors of the myth chose to minimize or overlook. Out of every 10,000 gainfully oc-cupied persons, 1858 were farmers. Their purchasing power had dropped from $4481 million in 1918 to $2888 million in 1921; these figures represent dollars having the same value as in 1913. After 1922 there was a slight average gain in farmers' incomes, but only a slight one. Over 250,000 farmers and their families were forced to give up their calling and move to the cities within five years. Nearly half the farmers, those whose land had a rela-tively low value, had no gain whatever over their prewar standards of living.

Bituminous coal mining and textiles—two of the greatest single industries—were suffering chronic depression; both coal miners and cotton-textile workers were, at the end of the period, receiving lower wages on the average than when "prosperity" began. A study of income in *Recent Economic Changes*, made under the direction of the National Bureau of Economic Research, set forth the conclusion that sections of the country comprising somewhat less than half the population—the East North Central, the Middle Atlantic, and the Pacific Coast regions—were the only ones in which an average gain of income had occurred; the other regions—New England, the South, the Middle West, and the Mountain States—had not, on the average, shared in prosperity at all.

As for the economy of high wages, the figures show that the largest average increase in purchasing power had taken place at a time when employers and bankers had been doing their best to keep wages down. During the 1920-1922 depression the effort was to "deflate" wages because prices were falling. As a matter of fact, employers were unable to reduce wages as fast as prices fell, and the result was that when full employment returned in 1923 the workers could buy considerably more than in 1920. When it was seen that this increase in real wages coincided with active business, the doctrine of the economy of high wages gained its vogue. In spite of this doctrine, the average manufacturing worker's yearly income was reduced $55 between 1923 and 1928, according to Dr. Willford I. King. The average miner's yearly income dropped $184 between 1922 and 1927. The only wage gains during this period were made in industries where, regardless of any advance in productivity, or regardless of the employers' attitude, the labor organizations were strong—railroads, building construction, printing, clothing. Meanwhile there was a disturbingly large volume of unemployment, not accurately known, but estimated by Dr. Leo Wolman at a minimum of 1,500,000 for even the most prosperous years, and rising to not less than 2,315,000 in 1927.

Nor did the public benefit by lower prices as a result of technical gains, to anything like the extent which those gains would have warranted. Though precise figures to support this conclusion are lacking, it is a reasonable inference from the fact that the prices of manufactured goods showed no great drop; they did not fall nearly so much as those of raw materials, to say nothing of following downward the reduced costs indicated by the figures of high productivity per man-hour. This conclusion is reinforced by the enormous and rapid growth of industrial profits. The gains of technology went, in the main, not to increased incomes for wage-earners, recipients of salaries, or farmers, or to reduced prices, but to larger profits.

Rapidly expanding consumers' credit, largely in the form of installment selling, did enable the great public for a while to enlarge its purchases of the growing volume of goods produced. But, with cash incomes failing to increase, there was a limit to the expansion of credit which could be extended to consumers. The limit appears to have been reached in 1928 and 1929. The careless mortgaging of future income dwindled when that future income arrived and was found to be little if any larger than the income previously received.

And the final symbol of prosperity—general sharing of industrial profits by speculation in stocks—turned out to be a delusion. Nobody knows how many stockholders there were at the peak of the speculative mania, but the belief that they included every elevator boy and bootblack was undoubtedly fallacious. There were far fewer than was generally supposed. Millions of farmers and industrial workers never had enough surplus to indulge in this pastime. Of course the great avalanche of the years 1929 to 1932 wiped out the gains of those who thought they were getting rich.

CHAPTER 5

The End of the New Era

The administration of President Harding and, after his death, that of President Coolidge adopted a passive, traditional policy. The federal budget would be balanced, and at a relatively low level, since taxes would be reduced from the high wartime rates. Business enterprise would be left to its own devices; there would be a minimum of government interference. Though neither President was versed in economic theory, the abandonment of economic planning could be justified by the classical doctrine of laissez faire as outlined by Adam Smith. In spite of all the shadows in the economic picture, the outcome until 1929, on the surface at least, seemed to justify the policy.

During the Harding-Coolidge era the index of wholesale prices (1926 = 100) never fell below 95 or rose above 104. The index of industrial production rose steadily; by 1929 it was one-third larger than in the boom year of 1920. National income, which rose from $56.5 billion in 1921 to $87.1 billion in 1929, was growing faster than the population.

The administration took a few positive steps to assist the economy. It directly subsidized the new aviation industry and American merchant shipping, while indirectly it helped along the rapid growth in the manufacture of automobiles by financing interstate highways. However, it steadfastly refused to give government aid to the farmers, who suffered from the fact that agricultural prices had fallen much farther than the prices of goods that farmers had to buy. And it was either indifferent or hostile to the attempts of labor to organize unions and bargain with employers.

In two crucial areas of policy, one domestic and the other international, the Republican administration departed from classical theory and, in effect, planted time-bombs that in the course of events would help to wreck economic growth. If Adam Smith could have assessed the policies of the national administration, he might well have asked two basic questions. First, what has happened to free competition in business and its role in pricing and distribution of income? Second, how can you justify a high protective tariff to hamper imports, while at the same time you insist that foreigners pay their debts to you?

More Inequality in the Distribution of Income

For many years a large part of the American people had attempted, without much success, to prevent monopoly or monopolistic practices in American industry. The Sherman Antitrust Act of 1890 had not been effectively enforced, as we have seen, largely owing to the ingenuity that big business had shown in controlling prices by methods that the courts held to be legitimate. President Theodore Roosevelt, stimulated by the Progressive movement of the early 1900s, had made futile efforts to eliminate the "bad" trusts. President Wilson in 1914 obtained passage of the Clayton Act, designed to close loopholes in the Sherman Act, and the Federal Trade Commission Act, intended to prevent the growth of monopoly by forbidding monopolistic practices before they could do damage. Neither statute could be rigorously enforced during the economic organization made necessary by World War I; and later the Harding-Coolidge administrations exerted almost no effort to demand compliance with any of these laws. Big business flourished; small business declined. Even in those industries which were not ruled by one or a few great corporations, Secretary of Commerce Herbert Hoover encouraged the activities of trade associations, which the war had stimulated. He helped them to carry out engineering standardization of their practices and the simplification of sizes, styles, and designs—reforms which represented great gains in efficiency but which at the same time made it easier for competitors to prevent "cutthroat competition" and thus to avoid recourse to price reductions as a means of augmenting their sales.

Between 1919 and 1930 combinations or purchases of business concerns accounted for the disappearance of more than eight thousand firms in manufacture and mining; before 1928 almost five thousand public utilities became parts of larger aggregates. Ultimately ten holding companies controlled 72 per cent of the sales of electric power. Chain stores, by 1929, had control of about one-fourth of retail sales.

At the end of 1929 two hundred companies possessed nearly half the corporate wealth, 38 per cent of the business wealth, and one-fifth of the total wealth of the nation. They did not, on the whole, increase selling prices, but neither did they reduce them. On the whole, costs declined because of gains in output per unit of labor. The index of man-hours per unit of product in manufacture declined from 67 in 1920 to 42 in 1929; in railroads and mining similar increases in productivity occurred. Employees gained in earnings per worker about 15 per cent between 1922 and 1929; property income in the same period was enlarged more than 41 per cent. Dividends paid were more than twice as large in 1929 as in 1922: the figures are, for 1922, $2962 million; for 1929, $6117 million. It does not seem likely that, taking the nation as a whole, the owners of business would have increased their incomes between two and three times as much as the gains in wage payments of their employees if competition had been as prevalent as Adam Smith thought it ought to be.

Calculations of the national income and its distribution, by Simon Kuznets, indicate that between 1923 and 1929 the individuals who received the highest 1 per cent of the national income gained 19 per cent in income; those who received the highest 5 per cent gained 14 per cent. Income-tax reductions during the same period were largest in the highest brackets. The net tax gain for those receiving incomes of $5000 was 1 per cent; those with incomes of $100,000 gained 10 per cent; those with $5 million incomes gained 27 per cent; and those with incomes of $1 million gained 31 per cent.

Stimulus for National Income

The inequalities in distribution of income during the 1920s did not involve absolute reduction of the smaller earnings. Almost all citizens made some gains—except farmers and those in the depressed industries—and there was little unemployment; but the rich gained more than the poor. They were enabled to do so because of unusual opportunities for investment.

One of those opportunities was the rapid expansion of relatively new industries. Before and during the war, only the few possessed automobiles. During the 1920s the industry grew like a weed and managed to sell more cars to families who did not have enough ready cash to pay for them, by use of borrowed money, payable on the installment plan. Before the end of the war no citizen owned a radio set; radio communication was a military secret. After it, almost every family bought one, and broadcasting became big business. Rayon and other synthetic fibers opened another gigantic retail market.

Perhaps an even greater stimulus was a postwar boom in construction, greatly strengthened by the demand for dwellings, which had not been built during the war. This upswing of construction began in 1920; it did not start to fall until about 1927. Economists believe, on the basis of careful study, that there are "long swings" in construction, of some fifteen to twenty years from peak to peak, and that they exert a strong influence on the state of the economy.

The growth of automobile manufacture and other factory industries of course stimulated the demand for machinery, machine tools, and the metals of which they are made; the construction boom increased the demand for a large variety of materials. Accompanying the new housing, manufacture of new household electrical devices such as refrigerators, vacuum cleaners, and kitchen ranges provided immense markets for manufacturers of electrical equipment.

Speculation

Speculation in land had been, for more than a century, a practice of Americans who wished to accumulate wealth quickly. Frequently the speculator borrowed from banks to finance his operations. When real-estate prices did not rise as he expected, and even more when they fell, he suffered heavy losses. During the boom of the 1920s this old practice was revived, not only for speculative housing projects or commercial buildings, but for investment in Florida, which was expected to boom because of the rapidly increasing wealth of the propertied classes and the general ownership of motor vehicles. As usual, the amateur speculators, dazzled by the prospect of easy riches, failed to look hard at the property they were buying, and often found themselves in possession of land which was under water or was not likely to be populated for decades. The Florida speculative balloon soon collapsed.

In the meantime many nonprofessional investors discovered that they could make easy money by buying shares on the stock exchanges. Profits and dividends were rapidly increasing, and the prices of common stock steadily rose (as a whole). The average increase was 176 per cent between 1923 and 1929. What more easy and pleasant way to accumulate riches than to buy shares which, on the average, were almost certain to rise in price? The number of shares traded increased steadily, except for a slight drop between 1925 and 1926. In 1923 the number of shares traded was 236 million; in 1929 it had become 1125 million. As long as the price of stocks rose, it was safe to borrow money with which to buy them. Why limit your purchases to $1000, which you took from the savings bank or obtained by selling your government bonds, when your broker would gladly lend you as much as $9000 more (thus of course enlarging his commission)? Trading on margin was almost routine, and its prevalence continually pushed market prices higher.

Of course the "insiders" did not refrain from using their power and their skills to collect for themselves much of the gains of the amateurs. They engaged in mergers, the formation of holding companies, and similar practices, keeping a sure profit in fees or special classes of securities which they alone held, while they peddled new issues to the public. By "rigging" the market they could push down the prices of shares which they wished to buy, or push up those which they wished to sell. They were expert in starting rumors which were in accordance with their plans of action. Of course the stock market, a central organ of private enterprise, was not under government regulation. Some prominent market operators got into trouble with the law by ordinary dishonesty, but, on the whole, the amateur traders who eventually lost more than they had gained had no legal redress.

New securities for sale on the market rose steadily from $4304 million in 1923 to $10,183 million in 1929. Estimates indicate that the 1923 issues equaled 29 per cent of the year's savings by the people of the nation, and in 1929 represented 50 per cent. Obviously the individual speculators for the rise were risking a large part of their current savings by buying new and untried issues. And margin trading had become widespread because of the usual increase in the market prices of stocks. In early 1929 the purchaser needed to advance only 10 per cent of the price (known as a ten-point margin), and his broker loaned him the other 90 per cent. The loan was payable when the collateral was sold. Of course the borrower had to pay interest on the loan, and the interest rates were high. The broker had the privilege of "calling" the loan at his pleasure. The "owner" of the stock had to pay on call, or the lender would take possession of the stock and sell it to recoup his advance. In March 1929, call loans earned 12 per cent, and the rate subsequently rose in three steps, to 15, 17, and 20 per cent. It is strange that speculators did not foresee the ruin which must come if, for any length of time, the market prices of securities should fall instead of rising. That time came in September 1929, and continued through the autumn. Like other speculative bubbles of history, this one burst when it could sail no higher.

A curious development occurred during the latter 1920s in the relations between business concerns and the banking system. So profitable had many firms become, and so large a share of the profits was retained by them, that they no longer needed to borrow much from their bankers. On the contrary, they deposited large sums in the banks, and many of the deposits earned interest. The banks came to depend, for a large share of their earnings, on loans to brokers, who in turn used the money in financing margin trading by their customers. When the Federal Reserve Board began to worry about the extent of margin trading and urged the commercial banks to diminish their loans to brokers, business concerns themselves advanced large sums to brokers, thus financing the speculation of the public in their own securities. It was indeed a curious state of affairs when corporations could make more money by lending their profits to speculators than by investing in larger production by industry.

Two opportunities remained for the bankers to sustain their earnings in the late years of the boom. One practice, used by some of the larger banks, was to organize and control subsidiaries which floated new securities by sales to investors, thus participating directly in the inflated money market. The other consisted of real-estate loans to speculators in land and buildings. A prominent architect told the author of this book that a builder in New York City could finance the construction of a new speculative building by a first-mortgage bank loan large enough to cover not only all his expenses but his profit. The builder did not have to risk any of his own funds. These two practices alone—flotation of risky bonds and high risking in real estate—are sufficient to illuminate the weakness of the banking system after the crash in 1929.

Obstacles to International Trade

Laissez faire, in the classical economic doctrine of Adam Smith, held that obstructions to trade across national boundaries are just as injurious to economic welfare and efficiency as obstructions within those boundaries. Why devote labor and capital to the production of any goods which could be bought more cheaply or were better in quality than the domestic product? It would be wiser for each nation to use its resources in production of things in which it held a comparative advantage. Competition among nations would be just as useful, in allocating resources and serving both the interest of the consumers and the wealth of the nations concerned, as was competition within a nation. But for many years the Republican Party in the United States, which never ceased extolling "competitive private enterprise," had supported a high protective tariff in order to rig the market in favor of American manufacture. True to its tradition, the Harding administration abandoned the relatively low customs duties which had been adopted by Wilson's Democratic Congress, and in 1922 passed the Fordney-McCumber Tariff Act, raising duties on manufactured goods to a level so high as to exclude many imports.

Before World War I, citizens of the United States owed more to foreigners than foreigners owed to them. British subjects and western Europeans had invested large amounts in American property, while Americans had invested abroad much smaller sums. As of July 1, 1914, Americans held foreign investments totaling $3514 million, while foreigners owned American securities and a balance of short-term credits for a total of $7200 million. (As has already been stated, there were no intergovernmental debts at the time.) The United States economy therefore was a debtor, and had to pay abroad more than it received in order to balance the net liabilities of $3686 million. The only way this could be done was by current sales abroad of goods and services exceeding payments for imports. A protective tariff which diminished foreign sale of manufactures to the United States could therefore be favored as a measure to cancel what was called an "adverse balance of payments."

The war, however, changed this situation radically. The United States no longer was a "debtor nation" but quickly became a creditor. On December 31, 1919, the net investments of foreigners in the United States had declined to less than zero; now American private investments abroad exceeded foreign private investments in the United States by $3985 million. In addition, the United States Government had loaned to the Allied and Associated nations a net sum of $9591 million. Thus, five years after the outbreak of war, the United States had become a creditor nation by the huge amount of $12,561 million.

The Harding-Coolidge administration insisted that the Allies must repay to the United States the money they had borrowed during the war. In almost the same breath, the administration proclaimed the necessity of erecting a high wall of protective tariffs to make it difficult for foreigners to sell their manufactures in the

United States. How, then, were the foreign debtors to obtain the dollars with which to pay their debts? Only ignorance could explain such a muddled policy. The champions of free, competitive private enterprise not only violated their own principles in favoring tariff protection, but also presented a seemingly insoluble problem to the international community. Indeed, they also declined to recognize that community when they prevented the United States from joining the newly founded League of Nations.

The record shows that in 1920, the year before President Harding took office, the United States imported merchandise valued at $5278 million, but that afterward, during the prosperous years culminating in 1929, yearly imports dropped in value by about a billion dollars. Other current payments to foreigners also fell by about the same amount. The value of United States exports was regularly larger, after 1920, than that of imports. How, then, could other nations pay for their current purchases in this country, to say nothing of their war debts?

Chiefly they were able to do so because Americans were investing large amounts in foreign nations. In the early years of the decade these investments consisted mainly of expansion abroad by American business concerns, which had large surplus earnings. In the later years a major portion of foreign investment by Americans was closely linked to the speculative mania on Wall Street. Investment bankers arranged foreign loans and peddled the securities—at a handsome profit for themselves—to the gullible and optimistic American customers of the brokers. Some of the loans were legitimate and safe so long as worldwide prosperity continued. Others verged on fraud.

A considerable amount of the new investments from the United States went to Germany, which could use the dollar proceeds to pay war reparations to France, which could then pay war debts to Britain. Then France and Britain could more easily pay the amounts needed to service the loans held by the United States Government and its citizens. The dollars came back to their place of origin. But when S. Parker Gilbert, in charge of reparations, warned against further lending in Germany, and when other foreign loans turned out to be unsafe, the house of cards tumbled.

Its fall contributed not only to the panic in Wall Street but to the depression that ensued. Bankruptcies in foreign countries intensified the collapse of the United States economy and were, by some American commentators, blamed for that collapse. Yet the principal source of the debacle could be traced to Wall Street, where the investment in foreign loans originated.

A Remnant of National Planning: Federal Reserve

One national planning institution—the Federal Reserve System, established in 1913 under President Wilson—was bequeathed to the Harding-Coolidge regime. In a real sense the system constituted a fulfillment of Alexander Hamilton's effort to establish a governmentally controlled central bank in order to curb inflationary speculation or, at other times, to pursue an "easy money" policy when the growth of the economy needed more financing. But the operation of the system proved to be less effective than Hamilton or its actual founders would have wished. During World War I it had been able to do little more than organize its activities and serve the government's need for funds. After 1920 it probably contributed to the absence of price inflation in markets for goods and services, and it was in part responsible for the mildness of two recessions, one in 1924 and the other in 1927. It could not, however, prevent the extravagant rise in stock-market speculation.

The legislation that created the Federal Reserve System was the outcome of Congressional investigations into money problems, after the collapses of previous speculative booms in the stock market and after the exposure of monopolistic practices by large private banks and insurance companies. Before the establishment of the system, it was the practice of local commercial banks to deposit their reserves in large private banking institutions in major cities, primarily New York. Interest was paid on the deposits by the big "bankers' banks." Since the deposits constituted reserves of the smaller banks, which might have to be withdrawn on demand, and since interest was paid on these deposits, a prevalent practice of the city banks was to invest them in call loans to brokers operating in the stock market. Under ordinary circumstances a withdrawal of deposits by a "country bank" could promptly be met by the calling of brokers' loans made by the city bank. But when, as had happened on several occasions, a panic occurred in the speculative market, and the depositary city banks could not liquidate the reserve deposits of their banking customers, the banking system might be in serious trouble, and for a time local depositors might not be able to cash their checks.

The new legislation established twelve Federal Reserve Banks, each covering a geographical area. All national banks were compelled by law to join the system, and state banks were allowed to do so. Each member bank bought shares in the Federal Reserve Bank of its district, and was entitled to dividends on its shares not exceeding 6 per cent. Each member bank was required to deposit its reserve in its Reserve Bank, with the exception of such cash as might be necessary for day-to-day operations. The reserves consisted largely of gold. The Reserve Banks could invest their capital, or deposits from member banks, only in government securities and the highly liquid "bankers' acceptances."

Six of the nine directors of each Reserve Bank were elected by the member banks of its district; only three of these could be bankers; the other three must be representatives of agricultural or business interests. Three directors of each Reserve Bank were chosen by a Federal Reserve Board in Washington, which supervised the whole system. Members of the Federal Reserve Board were appointed by the President of the United States; their terms of office were so staggered that no President could by his appointments gain control of the board. In the beginning the Secretary of the Treasury and the Comptroller of the Currency were members *ex officio*.

After the installment of the system, almost all the paper currency of the nation consisted of Federal Reserve notes, which superseded the old bank notes issued by hundreds of commercial banks. The Reserve Banks were by law required to maintain a gold reserve of not less than 40 per cent of the outstanding Federal Reserve notes. The gold reserve, at the same time, had to cover 35 per cent of all the reserves of the member banks.

Perhaps the most important function of the new system was to limit the loans of the commercial banks when price inflation threatened, and to make credit "easy" when a recession was feared. There were three ways in which these ends might be served.

One method depended on the power of the Reserve Banks to specify a minimum required ratio of the reserves of member banks to their outstanding loans. If a Reserve Bank wished to enlarge the amount of lending, it could reduce this required ratio; if it wished to curb bank loans, it could increase the ratio. This method is of little use in increasing commercial loans when the banks cannot find enough customers with good credit ratings—as in serious depressions—and it may be too rigorous in curbing expansion. It has seldom been used.

A second method depends on the "rediscount" interest rate. A member bank which has loaned money to a business concern or a farmer may borrow an equal amount from a Federal Reserve Bank by presenting to it the signed note or other legal document representing its customer's obligation. This note is added to the member bank's reserve, so that ability to lend is not diminished. Of course the member bank has to pay interest on the money it borrows. Decrease in the interest rate paid to Reserve Banks by borrowing banks may stimulate rediscounting and expansion of member bank loans, and vice versa. The effect of raising or lowering the rediscount rate is to raise or lower interest rates charged to commercial borrowers. This may or may not affect lending by member banks; the amount of demand for commercial loans may not be much influenced by small changes in interest rates.

The third method, not understood at the time the Federal Reserve System was created, is by far the most effective. It is called the "open market" policy. If the Reserve Banks wish to curb loans made by member banks, they can reduce the reserves of the member banks (identical with the deposits by member banks in Reserve Banks). Reserve Banks can do this by the simple expedient of selling government bonds on the "open" bond market. Purchasers of the bonds pay for them by drawing checks on the member banks where they keep deposits. These checks are, of course, made out to the selling Reserve Banks. The Reserve Banks then collect from the banks on which the checks are drawn. They do so by reducing the deposits of the member banks in the Reserve

Banks. These deposits by the member banks constitute their reserves; and reduction of their reserves curtails the ability of the member banks to lend. Exactly the opposite outcome follows purchase of bonds in the open market by the Reserve Banks.

In 1923 the *Federal Reserve Bulletin* set forth the major policies that the Reserve Banks have followed more or less faithfully since World War I. Briefly, the Reserve Banks favored expanding the volume of credit as long as it financed the growth of production, but would curb credit when the effect of expanding it would be a general increase in prices. The policies, as has been said, were of considerable value in dealing with mild recessions like those of 1924 and 1927, and in curbing minor threats of inflation. They proved grandly ineffective, however, both in the stock-market boom of 1927 to 1929 and in the major depression that followed it.

The Collapse of the New Era

In 1928 neither President Coolidge, whose term was about to expire, nor Herbert Hoover, who had just been elected to succeed him, entertained the slightest doubt that the United States economy was healthy. Coolidge said in his last message to Congress, dated December 4: "No Congress ever assembled, in surveying the state of the Union, has met with a more pleasant prospect than that which appears at the present time. . . . The great wealth created by our enterprise and industry, and saved by our economy, has had the widest distribution among our own people, and has gone out in a steady stream to serve the charity and business of the world. The requirements of existence have passed beyond the standard of necessity into the region of luxury. Enlarging production is consumed by an increasing demand at home and an expanding commerce abroad. The country can regard the present with satisfaction and the future with optimism."

A few months earlier, when Hoover was nominated for the Presidency in the summer of 1928, he said in his speech of acceptance, "We in America today are nearer to the final triumph over poverty than ever before in the history of any land." Scarcely anyone who was living at the time of his electoral campaign can forget his slogan: "A chicken in every pot, and two cars in every garage."

Not long after his inauguration, however, the Federal Reserve Board in the spring of 1929 warned the banks—and the public—of danger in the swelling amount of speculation for the rise in stock prices, financed by margin loans. The board did not then have the power—granted several years later—of regulating the percentage of margins allowable in call loans for purchase of stocks. Its warning in 1929 was not effectual. The scenes were set for the ensuing collapse of stock prices, bound to occur as soon as speculators or brokers should expect a major decline.

What actually started the downward movement is uncertain; there were numerous influences. One arose from the fact that so much British money had been attracted by speculative gains in the Wall Street market that the Bank of England lost too much gold and on September 26 increased its interest rate, thus attracting large amounts of money from New York. "Insiders" in the United States began to fear that speculating for the rise had been overdone, and sold shares to safeguard their winnings in the boom before it was too late. Others followed their lead. The stock market began to fall in September. The decline influenced still others to sell, and brokers began calling for more margin. If additional funds were not provided by customers, their stocks were dumped on the market. Already on October 15 stocks fell by an average of five or six points, and the decline continued the next day. In the brief session of Saturday, October 19, losses ranged from five to forty or more points. Whenever the market seemed to rally—as on Tuesday, October 22—speculators rushed to sell their securities in order to avoid the likelihood of further losses. Tuesday, October 29, was the climactic day when more than sixteen million shares changed hands and when the average price of fifty leading stocks, as compiled by *The New York Times*, declined by an average of almost forty points. The loss of values in two weeks had been the steepest in the history of the stock exchange. By November 13, when the market reached its lowest point for the year, the value of all listed stocks had fallen by about $30 billion.

President Hoover tried to calm the nation by asserting that these losses in stock speculation need have no effect on the economy as a whole. "The fundamental business of the country," he said "—that is, the production and distribution of goods and services—is on a sound and prosperous basis." Other American authorities denied that the speculative collapse would have any repercussion on business as a whole. Two leading British economists, Josiah Stamp and John Maynard Keynes, issued similar reassurances. Mr. Keynes pointed out that the bank credit which had financed the speculative purchase of securities would now be available for business engaged in the production and distribution of goods and services. Apparently he did not know that large American corporations had been lending, for brokers' loans, money which they did not need for their own operations. They had not been dependent on bank credit before the stock market collapsed.

Meanwhile there were substantial obstacles abroad to a resumption of the nation's former activity. World markets for wheat and cotton, depressed by unsold surplus stocks, opposed stubborn handicaps to agricultural prosperity. Worldwide collapse of credit and failing opportunities for foreign investment decreased or destroyed the markets for other products. Our prosperity, even while it lasted, had been an isolated phenomenon which was steadily being undermined by economic confusion outside our borders.

Thus the popular faith in business and the trust in prosperity lost its morale in a veritable debacle. The public, which had ignored other values, was betrayed by the gods it had chosen. It was no more happy or successful, in the end, than the minorities which it had despised. Its highroad had withered into an overgrown footpath through a seemingly impassable wilderness. The common fate of thwarted ambition had cast its shadow over everyone. The New Era furnished no dependable system within which people could live their lives. Advance into it was revealed not as progress, but as retreat. Bewilderment was universally acknowledged, and almost everyone felt the need of something really new.

CHAPTER 6

Hoover Fights the Depression

Long before Herbert Hoover first campaigned for the Presidency, the American public was familiar with his praiseworthy record. In World War I he presided over the Commission for Relief in Belgium, which provided food and clothing for civilians in that war-devastated country. When the United States entered the war, President Wilson called him home to be Food Administrator, a post which he occupied with outstanding success. Still later he had charge of famine relief in Central Europe and the Soviet Union. Many Progressive followers of Theodore Roosevelt would have been delighted if Hoover had been nominated for the Presidency in 1920, instead of the bumbling and unfortunate Warren G. Harding.

During the Harding and Coolidge administrations Hoover served as Secretary of Commerce, and he was a prominent figure in the New Era of the 1920s. He was then known as a management engineer, at a time when engineers were gaining renown by improving the efficiency of production. He aided several manufacturing industries by encouraging standardization and simplification, thus reducing waste and contributing to profits. Those appeared to be central problems in the prosperous years. It is important to note that Hoover was not a professional economist with a consistent body of theory. By talent and training he was tragically unequipped to deal with the central problems of the Great Depression. His chief aim as President, after the Wall Street crash of October 1929, was to revive the New Era of the 1920s, which he had previously served so well.

Attempted Aid to the Farmers

But the first economic measure of the new administration was enacted into law in June 1929, when prices in Wall Street were still rising toward their peak. It was a measure designed to help the farmers of the country, who had received no share of Coolidge prosperity. Indeed, hard times had begun for them with the sharp postwar recession of 1920 and 1921 and showed no sign of ending.

The farmers had been unusually prosperous during the war years because of the immense domestic and foreign demand for meat and grain. Many had bought additional land and agricultural machinery, usually on credit. In 1920 and 1921 the prices of crops fell much further than did the prices of everything that farmers had to buy, and the disparity persisted all through the 1920s. The farmers kept trying to obtain assistance from the federal government. A farm bloc in Congress made several attempts to raise crop prices by legislation, through bills introduced by Senator Charles L. McNary and Representative Gilbert N. Haugen. Whenever they succeeded in having one of their measures passed by Congress, President Coolidge vetoed the bill, and none was ever passed over his veto.

The chief proposal advocated by the farm bloc was to diminish the amount of agricultural products offered for sale in the United States in order to raise their prices. The aim was to bring crop prices to a level as much above that prevailing before the war as were the prices of other goods; the new level would be "parity." The method recommended for achieving it was to export as much of the major crops as would be necessary to hold the domestic supply to a quantity that would sustain "parity" prices. This type of farm relief came to be known as "the two-price system": a higher price for sales to domestic consumers, and a lower one for sales to foreign countries. All variations of the scheme required protective duties to prevent imports at prices below those maintained for American growers, and all would permit the sale of exported farm commodities at the lower world prices. Where the scheme varied was chiefly in the methods provided for stimulating agricultural exports.

During the Presidential campaign of 1928, the Republicans had promised to aid the farmers. Their attempt to fulfill the promise was embodied in the Agricultural Marketing Act, passed by the new Congress of 1929 as its first important measure and signed by the President on June 15. The act stipulated that the growers of each major crop should form a producers' cooperative, which would limit the output of its members. A national sales agency for each crop would control its marketing in order to maintain prices. A Federal Farm Board with capital supplied by the government would lend to each cooperative a sum equivalent to the expected proceeds of the sales. Governmental stabilization corporations would hold the crops in warehouses as collateral for the loans. When these stores were sold, the debts were to be canceled. "Surplus" crops, remaining after sales within this country at the fixed prices, would be sold abroad for whatever prices they would bring.

Such a plan was a long way from the ideal that Hoover shared with almost the whole business community, of "free, competitive, private enterprise." It might have worked in other circumstances, although a producers' cooperative with scores or hundreds of thousands of members could hardly exercise enough discipline over its widely scattered units to enforce a reduced volume of production. Any rise in price would almost certainly result in larger output. Paradoxically a fall in price would produce the same effect, since farmers would plant more in order to maintain their incomes.

No sooner had the project been organized than the collapse in Wall Street announced the Great Depression. Tax revenues and consumers' incomes shrank rapidly, and the $500 million appropriated for the Federal Farm Board soon approached exhaustion. Since the economic collapse was suffered by other nations as well as the United States, the foreign markets for American crops were beginning to vanish. Internally the index of wholesale prices for farm products fell by more than half, from 104.9 in 1929 to 51.4

in 1932 (1926 = 100). On the record, the entire project was a stunning failure.

Prosperity Was Not Around the Corner

When the stock market crashed in the fall of 1929, industrial depression was already a measurable phenomenon, both in this country and abroad. The crash was not the cause, much less the sole cause, of the depression; rather it was the most dramatic among many factors that intensified the depression after it was under way. Residential building had begun to slacken in 1928; industrial and commercial building in the spring of 1929. A decline in the production of automobiles started in June, and it was accompanied by a general slump in industrial production. The cumulative effect of such developments in the United States began to show in a fall of wholesale prices in July. Those prices had already started to decline in Europe: in France, by February; in Germany, Great Britain, Italy, and the Netherlands, by March. The wholesale prices of many commodities are set in a world market, and their fall in Europe was evidence of a shrinking world demand that was certain to be reflected in this country. Liquid funds had flowed from Europe in large quantities to augment our speculative boom. The withdrawal of such funds in October was among the direct causes of the debacle on the stock exchange. Some funds were withdrawn because the danger signals were more clearly recognized abroad than at home; others because the money was needed to pay the costs of the depression that was already felt in the countries from which the funds had come.

Wall Street needed only a slight push to topple the structure. When everybody is buying not for investment, but in the hope of selling again at higher prices, then everybody will sell when it becomes clear that prices are falling. A crash is inevitable.

It became a popular legend that Hoover had no plan to counteract the effects of the crash and that he did nothing except to wait for a return of prosperity, "just around the corner." Quite on the contrary, he had a very definite plan and acted promptly upon it. His conception of the affair was based on the opinion prevailing in the financial community: that the nation's business of production and trade was fundamentally sound, that the only trouble was a speculative collapse in the stock market, and that the main task was to insulate business against the loss of confidence that might follow the collapse. The only real enemy, he believed, was fear. He also believed that private business, disorganized and planless as it had proved itself to be, was the principal support of stability, instead of being a weak point in the structure. Therefore he called together the leaders of business and labor and asked them to proceed with their activities as if nothing had happened. Employers were to keep on expanding their plants, ordering their materials, producing, and selling. They were not to reduce prices or wages. Labor was not to rock the boat. Government, for its part, was to push ahead with public works. If everybody was assured that everybody else would act in this fashion, fear would be banished, confidence would prevail, and business would not lose its fundamental soundness.

Although the plan in retrospect seems pitifully inadequate, it was in consonance with the best judgment and prevailing opinion of those who exercised actual economic power in the nation. They controlled the party that elected Hoover, a large part of the press, and business and financial organizations throughout the country. The President was acting with their hearty approval, and, if their assumptions had been correct, his plan would have worked. Its utter failure proves not that Hoover was incompetent, but rather that the depression had deeper causes than the collapse of the stock market and that business could not, under its existing regime, cooperate for any such purpose as he set forth.

The business of production and trade was not fundamentally sound. Production could not be maintained because, in the circumstances, the goods could not be sold. Employment and wages could not be guarded against shrinkage. Markets had definitely been lost: markets abroad, for this nation had ceased lending there or buying as much as it should; markets at home for automobiles and houses and other durable goods, because a saturation point of sales had been reached in reference to the purchasing power of the ultimate consumers. Public works—of the sort that might be financed by a balanced budget, on which Hoover strongly

insisted in principle—could not be expanded sufficiently because
the government had not planned them in advance and had not accumulated enough funds to do the job quickly or on a large enough
scale. To cap the climax, few at the conference had any abiding
faith that others there would live up to their promises. There was
no binding obligation, in a competitive order, for anyone to do so.

The Tariff Again

In the spring of 1930 Congress was debating a new tariff bill. The
tariff had long been the Indian snake oil of the dominant industrial
interests. It was the patent remedy for everything. It had made
manufacturers rich, and manufacturers had made America rich.
Every depression had been caused—so the public was told—by
reducing it or by efforts to reduce it. Now, in their extremity and
fear, business representatives in Congress returned to it as a dying
sinner returns to his childhood faith.

Under the Smoot-Hawley Tariff Act as it finally took shape,
import duties were, on the average, between 53 and 59 per cent of
the value of the import. Apparently a majority of the legislators believed that raising duties to their highest point since 1830 would lift
the nation miraculously out of the depression. Almost the whole
body of qualified economists thought otherwise. In a statement
signed by 1028 members of the American Economic Association,
including both liberals and conservatives on the faculties of all the
big universities, they called on the President to veto the Smoot-
Hawley bill if it passed Congress. They said that European nations
could not pay their war debts or the interest on their loans from
American bankers, or buy the goods produced by American farms
and factories, unless we bought European goods in return. Hoover
promised to take their statement under consideration. On June 16,
however, he announced that he was signing the bill. The news
produced what *The New York Times* called "a torrent of liquidation," affecting the whole stock market and leading to the broad-
est and steepest decline in values since November 1929.

If Americans had had the wish to buy goods from abroad and
the means to do so, the Smoot-Hawley Act would have proved a
mighty obstacle. On the record, the total value of American im-

ports fell by more than half between 1929 and 1933. The loss of
sales in the American market by producers in Europe embarrassed
great international banks, which had already suffered from the
losses of their customers who speculated in Wall Street. For this
and other reasons the Creditanstalt in Vienna had to close its
doors in May 1931; other banks in Berlin and elsewhere on the
Continent fell over like dominoes. Many nations retaliated by increasing their own tariffs. This obstacle to exports from the United
States, plus the worldwide depression, was responsible for a fall
in United States exports from about $6 billion in 1929 to hardly
$1 billion in 1934. World imports fell in the same period from
nearly $35 billion to nearly $10 billion.[1] In Great Britain and on
the Continent many believed that their economic plight was caused
by the depression in the United States. President Hoover, on the
other hand, later blamed Europe for the long continuance of the
depression, since Europeans could not pay their debts to this country. American economists, after urging Hoover to veto the tariff
bill, felt that his refusal to follow their advice had been as disas-
trous as they expected it to be.

The Downward Spiral

In spite of all promises an efforts to maintain production, one
menacing fact made it impossible to do so. *Goods could not be
sold as fast as they were made.* After a short time of producing
ahead of orders, any businessman could see the result in his own
stockrooms. A prominent statistical concern sent questions to a
large number of corporations concerning the growth of their inventories during 1929. Between the beginning and the end of that
year, stocks of unsold goods were reported to have increased as
follows:

	(Per cent)
Office equipment	13
Copper	15
Retail stocks	16
Iron and steel	18

[1] Ilse Mintz, *American Exports during Business Cycles, 1879-1958.* National
Bureau of Economic Research, 1961.

	(*Per cent*)
Agricultural machinery	22
Oil	22
Electrical equipment	27
Foods	30
Railroad equipment	35
Household products and supplies	40

Meanwhile individual consumers had, by the million, ceased replacing the stocks of durable or semidurable goods which they had bought: automobiles, houses, rugs, furniture, and even clothing. In these circumstances manufacturers could not and did not keep their promises to maintain production.

Many economists believed that the government could stimulate business and employment by a large program of public works. Construction is a great industry which, when it is busy, employs many workers and orders materials from many other industries. The decline of construction after 1926 was a major influence in bringing on the depression. According to subsequent estimates by Simon Kuznets, the investment in new construction (in 1929 dollars) declined by $1580 million between 1926 and 1929. The decline continued more rapidly to 1933, with a total loss of expenditure for the period of more than $9 billion. This was something more than a loss of confidence. Public works financed by the federal government might have replaced some of the missing expenditure. But President Hoover believed that an essential cornerstone of confidence is a balanced budget, no matter how diminished the public revenues might be. He would not borrow to stimulate the building trades.

Another tragic waste was the downward spiral of payments to wage-earners in general. As the depression continued, millions were laid off or put on part time. Most of those who retained their jobs suffered from a series of wage reductions. There was no legal minimum wage. We have seen that during the prosperous years many persons, including employers, had praised the "economy of high wages," the doctrine which held that an increase in wage earnings enlarged the market for a rising output of goods and so increased the wealth of all. The reverse occurred during the depression. The reduction of wage earnings reduced sales, diminished or eliminated profits, and led to more layoffs and more wage reductions. Private enterprise could not reverse the process. Competitors did not dare to risk hiring more workers while the market sagged; monopolies had nothing to gain by raising wages. The outcome was a continued slide into depression for all, a vicious spiral to which there seemed to be no bottom.

Private philanthropy and local public relief tried to feed, clothe, and house the destitute unemployed, but the task was too great for those agencies. Often they could do little more than maintain breadlines. To supply the unemployed with enough cash so that they could buy even a minimum of essentials was far beyond their ability. Meanwhile aid from the federal government was precluded by a delusion that persisted at the time, especially among the well-to-do. The delusion was that, while certain unfortunate people always need help, and at some times more people need help than at others, the obligation to help them is not a social one, but merely the moral imperative of private generosity on the part of those who feel charitable. Furthermore, that there are always enough charitable people, of small means and large, to succor the needy. They felt that it is all right to "give until it hurts," but decidedly wrong to be taxed until it hurts, if the taxes are used to repair the human damage of a broken-down industrial system.

This delusion was shattered against the fact that a considerable proportion of the necessary relief had to be shouldered by local governments and paid out of taxes from the beginning; as time went on, much more than half the relief came from these public sources. The delusion threw the burden first on the relatives and friends of the unemployed, in city and country, who could least afford it and had least responsibility for the crisis, and then on local governments dependent for income on property-owners already groaning under the weight of local taxes.

President Hoover conscientiously rebuffed all requests that the federal government come to the aid of unemployment relief. One of his motives for refusing them was his insistence that a basic requirement for economic recovery was the sort of business confidence that he thought would be maintained by a balanced budget. But he also had moral scruples which, in August 1932, he declared as follows:

> It is not the function of the government to relieve individuals of their responsibilities to their neighbors or to relieve private institutions of their responsibilities to the public, or of local government to the states, or of state governments to the federal government. It is only . . . by this insistence upon individual responsibility, that there accrue great sums of individual accomplishment which carry the nation forward.

To many citizens this seemed strange doctrine from a man who had won much of his prestige by successfully managing war relief, financed by United States federal funds, of European people whose resources had been critically diminished by invasion. Meanwhile the President's fiscal policy prevented federal aid to the destitute, which might have helped to enlarge consumer purchasing power and so to check in some degree the downward spiral of workers' incomes and the sale of goods. "Rugged individualism" could not check the social ills that beset the nation's economy.

For a statistical picture of the depression, it is enough to give a very few figures. Gross National Product fell from $103.8 billion in 1929 to $55.8 billion in 1933, that is, by almost half. The disposable personal income (that is, after paying taxes) per capita of the population shrank from $678 in 1929 to $360 in 1933. When these figures are modified by price declines of consumer goods to show "real" per-capita income, the purchasing power per person fell from $936 in 1929 to $659 in 1933, in terms of 1949 dollars.

In 1929 aggregate corporate profits were $10.3 billion. In 1932 corporations had a net loss of $2 billion—after eliminating the decline in inventories due to depreciation, and after payment of taxes.

Owners of farms had incomes totaling $5.7 billion in 1929. In 1932 they earned only $1.7 billion.

Unemployment is difficult to measure for those years, largely because there was no system of governmental employment agencies. The best estimates indicate, however, that in 1929 about

1,550,000 persons, or 3.2 per cent of the civilian labor force, were unemployed, whereas in 1933 the unemployed numbered 12,830,000, or 24.9 per cent of the civilian labor force. The labor force contains not only wage-earners, but recipients of salaries, professional men who are self-employed, and the individual proprietors of small firms. The ratio of unemployment among wage-earners was higher—in some cities, such as Detroit, it was much higher—than in the civilian labor force as a whole.

CHAPTER 7

American Planners
and the Russian Experiment

As the months of dreary recession passed without any sign of recovery, many Americans proposed new policies. Few advocated, or even expected, that the "working class" in this country would produce a revolution such as the one which had occurred in Russia, where the state had taken possession of industry and agriculture and then had found it necessary to impose a comprehensive plan governing the production and distribution of goods and services. Nevertheless there were numerous suggestions for a more orderly procedure in the United States than that which had led to the collapse of the New Era. There were, in our own history and culture, developments which seemed to lead to more rational and more manageable economic institutions. Suggested methods of planning came from a variety of sources, including business organizations, academic scholars, and the anti-Communist American Federation of Labor. Let us first look briefly at the contribution of the management engineers to the concept of economic planning.

Scientific Management

The application of conscious organization to a limited realm of endeavor is illustrated by the school of management engineering which in the United States was formally inaugurated by Frederick W. Taylor and which later was called "scientific management." By means of intelligent analysis and careful measurement, it broke through the crust of custom which had grown up in manufacturing establishments. Naturally enough, its first point of attack was the job of the individual worker. Was he doing it in the best possible way? Did he have the best possible tool or machine? What time ought he to take in each operation? Repeated observations and experiments, called "time and motion study," discovered the most efficient methods of work and established the tasks which ought to be expected if the job were done in this way. Jobs were carefully analyzed and responsibilities were fixed. The story of how this made possible great increases of output and eliminated wastes is an old one.

The workers, not understanding the object of the study, and fearing that it was simply a method of making them work harder without increased rewards, at first opposed it as a way of making machines out of men, a new device of exploitation, an insult to human dignity. The scientific managers learned that without the cooperation of the workers their best efforts were largely ineffective. In some cases they were able to gain this cooperation by convincing the workers that they could expect to share the benefits of increased efficiency. In many cases the stupidity of employers, or the competitive forces outside the single establishment, prevented any such assurance, and the work of intelligent management was vitiated at the first step.

Scientific management did not have to go far before it discovered that its task was not to centralize authority, not to bend the wills of many to the will of one, but to coordinate the activities of all concerned in a way dictated by the requirements of the situation. The final authority was not the human boss but the nature of machine industry. And scientific management assumed that the purpose of machine industry was to produce as much as possible with as little effort as possible. It assumed that everyone concerned would have a mutual interest in achieving this objective, and hence that the essential cooperation in an ordered and scientific method of production could be achieved. Since these assumptions were not entirely valid, under the business regime, scientific management was unable to fulfill anything like its full ambition.

From the individual worker, the engineers went on to coordination of the several departments of the plant. They elaborated procedures for seeing that materials and semi-finished products flowed along the shortest possible routes, and in correct quantities so that blockades would not occur. They attended to the proper methods of hiring and firing, the intelligent selection and treatment of personnel. They eliminated organizational wastes of many sorts. They devised apt systems of cost finding and accounting control. They developed the distinction between the "line" function of executive responsibility and the "staff" functions of research, planning, and communication. They turned their attention not merely to production, but to purchasing and selling. They worked out methods of administration for large industrial organizations having many units, so that their parts could be harmonious. They discovered which activities must be centrally controlled, and which must be decentralized in order to avoid bureaucratic stagnation.

During the second winter of the Great Depression, the Taylor Society, devoted to the principles of scientific management, held a discussion of certain propositions drawn up by its managing director, Dr. H. S. Person. These propositions were not set forth as the final conclusion either of the society or of Dr. Person, but they were an admirable condensation of what many engineers were thinking and saying. They set forth that "the operations of industrial society are not yielding substantial good to the greatest number of industrial citizens. This is because these operations are not . . . organized with that end in view." More particularly, it is "because of an inconsistency between the basic principle of business enterprise—*individual self-interest and intuition*—and the basic principle of the production technology which that enterprise, without full appreciation of its influence, has come to use—*cooperative integration.*" Failure to extend the latter principle is what causes dislocations of industrial processes, unemployment, and the halt in our progress. This type of observation, the memorandum continues, is not new; better-organized societies have many times been proposed. But the suggested utopias have not been in accord with the possibilities presented by the technologies of their times. What is new in the present is "industrial technology, which has undergone great and rapid change during the past half century." New principles of organization and control of individual enterprises have been invented and tested. "If these were applied to the organization and control of industrial society, conceived as an organic whole, many and perhaps most of the forces which now cause periodic dislocations and distress in industrial life would be eliminated."

Although an individual enterprise may be stabilized in its internal adjustments, "the internal stability of an enterprise established by scientific management is frequently nullified by the impact of forces of the industrial environment outside the control of management." There is an increasing interdependence among "individuals, enterprises and groups. These organic inter-relationships are so intricate and delicate in their adjustments as to expose the industrial organism at any one of numerous points to maladjustment which is reflected all along the line of inter-relationships."

The main reason for these maladjustments, Dr. Person wrote, is that the task of adjustment among industrial units and groups is left to "the chance composite influence of a vast number of enterprises motivated by individual gain in competitive activities, limited in their perception of relationships and the organic consequences of their activities, and on the whole dependent upon intuition for their decisions as to purpose and method." This was the engineer's description of what the traditional economist flatteringly called "natural economic forces." The established social mechanisms on which industry is dependent, like currency and credit, were likewise uncoordinated.

The obvious conclusions were that the problem must be recognized, that an industrial self-government must be created which would involve "greater limitation to individual freedom in business activities than is at present assumed to be desirable," and that the principles of scientific management developed in individual enterprises must be applied "to industry conceived as one vast enterprise in which all members of industrial society are workers and share-holders in common."

It was in this fashion that the organizing man extended his ideas to grapple with the confusion of an unmanaged economy. What was here said by the engineer in careful and abstract form was being said every day in some way or other by people at every level of society. In many places there was recognition of the disparity between the marvelous efficiency of industrial technique and the

clumsy, destructive behavior of economic society as a whole. Why
was there too much wheat while people went hungry? Why, if we
had learned to perform such marvels of production, need anyone
be unemployed or poor? What was the matter with the way we
used our machines? The idea arose so logically out of the situation
that it was bound to become a leading idea; it had a natural con-
tagion. What gave it the ring of reality, in contradistinction to former utopian proposals, was, as Dr. Person shrewdly observed, that
now we had the necessary technique; we had seen and proved on
a small scale what it could do.

Meanwhile it seemed to many that the Russians were pointing
the way toward a direct intervention of government in production
and distribution.

The Russian Experiment in Planning

The years of civil conflict in Russia, during which the forces under the influence of Lenin established their dictatorship, generally
known as "War Communism," could not be an era of enlarged production. Reliable statistics for national output in this disturbed
period do not exist, but there can be little question that it was far
below that of 1913, before the European war. About the only
economic control that the new regime could exercise, aside from
the "liquidation" of persons regarded as enemies of the revolution,
was a rationing system to distribute whatever consumers' goods
could be found.

It is conservatively estimated that between 1913 and 1920, the
last year of the civil war in Russia, the nation's industrial production shrank by about 80 per cent, while agricultural output fell
about 50 per cent. Famine and epidemic diseases reduced the population by approximately 5 million.

In 1920 Lenin adopted a temporary measure to encourage production; it was called the New Economic Policy (NEP). For the
time being it permitted private enterprise as a means of relieving
the many scarcities. This use of the profit incentive was contrary
to Marxist principles, but Lenin described it as taking a step backward in order to make possible two steps forward. It worked. Production began to rise, and by 1928 it had reached about the same

level as that of 1913. Much of it, clearly, was not socialist production.

Marxist theory, which the Communist Party under Lenin always intended to put into practice—with some additions—demanded that the means of production should be removed from private ownership and taken over by the state (or else by cooperatives which the workers controlled). This change would, in theory, transfer from the capitalist class to the proletariat the "surplus value" (profits) previously claimed by the employers.

Obviously this revolution would not meet the future requirements of the nation if the profits of each firm were simply used to increase the wages of its employees, or were distributed to them in the form of dividends. It might be presumed that the recipients would have little incentive to devote their share of the profits to investment in new enterprises or undeveloped industries, but instead would attempt to increase their own consumption. Since there would be little or no capital left to finance new enterprises, the principal result would be rising prices for consumer goods, the makers of which in turn would reap more profits and distribute more dividends to themselves, a process that would almost inevitably lead to a vicious circle of inflation. The process could be avoided, under socialism, only if the state exercised a close control over consumption and investment.

Partly this explains the economic background of the first Five Year Plan. It should also be noted, however, that Russia possessed many of the requisites for large-scale industrialization. The natural resources of the nation were ample. It was second only to the United States in known sources of petroleum; it produced 90 per cent of the world's output of platinum (as well as an unknown percentage of the gold), and it led in the production of manganese. There were great unexplored deposits of other minerals, notably iron ore and copper. Large forests were a source of timber and furs. The Soviet state, which maintained a monopoly of foreign trade, tried to attract capital by offering concessions to exploit some of these riches; but this again was regarded as a temporary expedient and a step backward from socialism.

Russia also possessed some resources in point of industrial organization. Before the First World War, manufacturing in the regions of St. Petersburg (later called Leningrad), Moscow, and the Ukraine was for the most part concentrated in large plants employing more than a thousand workers each; their employees constituted nearly half of the factory workers in the nation. Their executive staffs, however, consisted largely of German or English managers, and these had disappeared in the course of hostilities. Industrial equipment had always been imported, and it was wearing out. The transport system of railroads, highways, and waterways was in dire need of repairs and expansion.

Soviet Russia, in short, was an underdeveloped nation. Even if one should ignore the desire of its leaders to construct more military equipment in order to protect the country from invasion, the emphasis was naturally on rapid growth of the heavy manufacturing, transportation, hydroelectric power, and mining industries, even at the expense of individual consumers. The state, as the owner of producing institutions, in 1928 set as its aim the efforts to "overtake and surpass" the relatively high output of the United States economy. To do so, the leaders thought, would require a national plan to guide the performance of the producing institutions in an economy completely governed by the state. A new state planning commission, often referred to as "Gosplan," worked out a five-year plan, the first of a long series. The businessmen who had taken advantage of the New Economic Policy—generally known as "Nepmen"—soon disappeared, if not in person, at least as private capitalists. The government adopted the plan and took the drastic measures which seemed necessary to execute it.

Repercussions in the United States

At the cost of immense sacrifices, the first Five Year Plan succeeded brilliantly in some fields and failed tragically in others. Perhaps the most important success was in the field of heavy machinery and equipment, where new plants were built and a whole new working force was trained, so that Russia was prepared for World War II. The tragic failure was in agriculture, where the peasants' rebellion against being forced into collective farms (combined with Stalin's decision to let them starve) produced the famine of 1932. But this disaster owed to miscalculation was not widely discussed in the United States, where the many lesser failures of the plan were also viewed with tolerance. The feature of it that impressed American observers was that everybody had a job in Russia and every industry was being expanded year by year instead of being caught in a deepening spiral of depression.

The Soviet Union, in its efforts to fulfill the plan, requested and obtained the services of many American management engineers. None of these proved willing to accept Communist political dogma, but many of them were impressed by the possibilities of national planning. Returning to the United States in the depths of the depression, they felt that this country might in its own way utilize its immense resources and idle manpower by planning within the framework of the capitalist system. Much public interest was aroused by the enthusiastic reports of some of the returned engineers. In 1931 a book about Russian planning, *New Russia's Primer*, by M. Ilin, was one of the more popular monthly choices of the Book-of-the-Month Club.

Many suggestions for an American system of planning were published at the time. We had from Stuart Chase a suggestion for a Peace Industries Board that would parallel the War Industries Board of 1918, and from the historian Charles A. Beard a suggestion for industrial syndicates under a National Economic Council, regulated under the theory of public-utility control and supplemented by planning agencies for agriculture, public works, foreign trade, and the rebuilding of cities. A committee of the National Progressive Conference, convened early in 1931, published a memorandum on "Long Range Planning for the Stabilization of Industry." Schemes for planning by separate, autonomous industries according to the principle of the trade association or cartel came from many business sources, notably from Gerard Swope of General Electric and from the United States Chamber of Commerce. The American Federation of Labor and other bodies came forward with a less detailed advocacy of national planning.

Unfinished Tools of Planning

Economic research in the 1920s had undertaken tasks which would be required for salutary national economic planning, but the work was far from completed when the Great Depression arrived.

In the early years of the decade the (nongovernmental) National Bureau of Economic Research put together the figures which we now know as Gross National Product, Net National Income, and the like. Knowledge of increases or decreases in these totals and the items that comprise them are necessary in adopting goals of national planning and checking success in reaching them. Yet the current figures were not routinely gathered and published by the United States Department of Commerce for many years after the models were perfected; nor did their nature and use penetrate the textbooks of economics used in the 1920s or even the 1930s. The lay public knew little or nothing about these basic measurements of income, spending, saving, and investment.

When the depression arrived, everybody knew that many workers lost their jobs, but in the late 1920s and early 1930s there were no accurate figures of the changes in employment and unemployment. The decennial census gathered data on the subject, but there were no regular totals from month to month or even from year to year. There could be no such totals without a comprehensive system of governmental employment agencies at which job-seekers could register, and those agencies did not exist until unemployment benefits were routinely paid under a system of compensation such as was to be adopted during the Franklin Roosevelt administration.

Other areas of the economy were better served with current data. The amount of money and credit, and an index of industrial production, were reported in the monthly Federal Reserve Bulletin. The Department of Agriculture supplied much information about crops and their prices. The Department of Commerce regularly published statistics of commodity imports and exports, though it was not until the late 1920s that it began compiling figures on the international balance of payments. Of course the Treasury Department reported on federal income and expenditures. But there was as yet no public agency to put together such current information in a manner that would throw light on the behavior of the national economy as a whole.

Although the necessary knowledge might have been created at the time, the organization necessary for national economic planning would still have been missing. It would not be established because the administration lacked the will to move in that direction. President Hoover had other plans.

CHAPTER 8

The Second Phase of Hoover Planning

When it became necessary to acknowledge that the first Hoover plan of holding the industrial status quo and injecting confidence had failed, there ensued a long, weary period of waiting. The country waited while production declined, prices fell, incomes shrank, the number of unemployed increased, mortgages were foreclosed, bank and insurance-company assets wore away, banks failed. The longer it tried to pump up confidence while these things went on, the less possible it was to have confidence. The confidence-pump squeaked and leaked, and finally stopped altogether. The administration waited for the "natural" end of the depression and the "natural" beginning of revival. Meanwhile its principal action was negative. It resisted all suggestions and agitations for more governmental activity. It turned a deaf ear to the growing clamor for enforcement of the anti-wage-reduction agreement, for some form of public unemployment relief, for a different kind of help to the farmers, and for a large public-works program based on borrowing. Although this last course had been endorsed by Hoover many years before when it had been suggested by economists as an anti-depression measure, and although he had actually inaugurated it in a small way in the first winter after the Wall Street disaster, he now turned against it because he was convinced that it was more important to balance the budget. The two things were in obvious contradiction. Anything he could do which involved large borrowing might weaken the securities market and discourage new private investment, and he relied upon private investment to start revival.

This was the period which gave rise most of all to the legend which spread in the early depression years, that the President was a spineless mass of jelly in the face of the nation's difficulty; that he was incapable of action. Yet he was still pursuing a definite policy, endorsed in theory both by the financially powerful and by the conservative economists. It was a slightly different one from that which he had attempted to practice at the beginning, and yet the two were related. The first theory had assumed that there was nothing much the matter, and that if everyone could be induced to believe this, there would be no danger. The second theory had to admit that there was something the matter: in some mysterious manner the system had got out of kilter. But the way to remedy the disease was to let it run its course without interference. The economic order was a self-compensating one and if left alone would get into balance. If wages were allowed to sink, that would reduce costs, profits would therefore reappear and furnish a bait for production, output would increase, and employment would turn up. Existing goods would wear out, inventories would reach a minimum, and finally simple necessity would require enlarged production. Disparities in prices would be corrected by the force of competition. Prices that were too high would be driven down. Inflated capital values would perforce be written off. The disappearance of weaker banks would strengthen the others. Eventually the banks would adjust their assets to lower values and begin to lend again. All that was necessary was for the politicians to keep hands off and resist agitation for action which might either interfere with these "natural" readjustments or frighten those who had money to lend and invest. This was the reason for trying to balance the budget and resisting the appeal for larger federal expenditure on any form of relief or construction.

There is a logical connection between this and the first policy, divergent though they were in their prescriptions. The first policy had assumed that no real danger was threatened, because it had always assumed that the system was self-compensating. If the economic order was naturally one that worked well, why expect serious difficulty? But when difficulty came, the trust in self-compensation dictated that no further "artificial" action be taken.

A negative program like this will very likely work, if given enough time and allowed to proceed to a conclusion. If production, employment, wages, prices, and capital values are allowed to sink low enough, a point will somewhere be reached at which a new balance of economic factors can exist and advance can begin. That point may be zero. It may be so far back that in order to regain it we must retrace the steps of half a century of business and financial development. But somewhere along the downward course it lies, even if it is so low that it demands a complete rebuilding of capitalism from the ground up.

What this theory does not anticipate is the social and political cost of a logical deflationary program. It does not see that on account of the powers of resistance which have been built up by concentrations of industry and capital, certain important prices and values will not be sufficiently deflated until the majority of the citizens have been reduced to a misery which they simply will not endure. It does not acknowledge the power which capitalist interests possess over the government itself, or foresee that they will use the government to prevent, if possible, their own deflation.

That is exactly what happened to Mr. Hoover's program. He was adamant against public relief of the unemployed, of the distressed farmers. He was adamant against unbalancing the budget for an employment-creating building program. But the time came when the financial shoe began to pinch too hard. Railroads, insurance companies, and banks were in danger. The better bonds might be defaulted. Deflation began to eat into the basic financial structure of private capitalism. At this point Hoover abandoned laissez faire and threw government credit into the breach. He did it because those who controlled railroads, insurance companies, and banks convinced him that it was necessary. They convinced him that if their wealth went, everything would go. Capitalist society, when the logical implications of a deflationary program began to be imminent, simply could not take it.

The result was that the government tried to protect the great capital hoards against the onslaught of the deflation which it was allowing to proceed unhampered in the earnings of workers, farmers, and business income in general. This was, in reality, gambling on the hope that a turning point would be reached before serious inroads had been made on fixed capital investments. But this gamble was increasing the rigidity of the most rigid element of the system while doing nothing to stop the decline of the most flexible. It was as if, when breaks appeared in a levee, the engineers should strengthen the parts which were already the strongest while doing nothing about the parts that were giving way. The business system was repeating an old mistake. In the name of laissez faire it was preventing action designed to help the more unfortunate, while it was calling upon government to employ deliberate interference with the free play of economic forces to protect the centers of economic power. The net result was to weaken itself.

The Reconstruction Finance Corporation

Two years after the stock-exchange panic, on December 8, 1931, the President asked Congress to establish a Reconstruction Finance Corporation to prevent the impending bankruptcies by lending governmental funds to banks and business corporations which could not find other credit. The RFC was designed as an emergency institution, to be liquidated in two years. Hoover said that "the very existence of such a bulwark will strengthen confidence." Congress passed the requisite legislation. The RFC received from the government a capital of $500 million, and it was permitted to issue tax-free debentures, guaranteed by the United States, of $1500 million. Its loans were to be kept secret in order to protect the credit status of the recipients.

The RFC opened agencies in thirty cities. At the end of its first year its outstanding loans amounted to nearly $1250 million, largely to banks and railroads. It was not liquidated in two years, but continued its operations throughout the subsequent regime of President Franklin D. Roosevelt. It was useful in financing military projects in World War II; its life was not terminated until the 1950s. It did not, however, prevent the banking crisis of 1932 and 1933.

One difficulty was the secrecy of its operations. Members of Congress, spurred by widespread opposition to the President's refusal to use federal funds for unemployment relief, argued that it was asking too much of the citizens for their government to give secret aid to large banking and business concerns. Ugly rumors charged that favoritism or corruption existed in choosing the recipients of the loans. Congress voted that the names of the borrowers be revealed; the President acquiesced with the proviso that, by a gentleman's agreement, only the members of the national legislature would see the list and that they would not share the knowledge with anyone else. This promise was broken in a subsequent debate, and the revelation doubtless harmed public confidence in the banks concerned.

Nevertheless it may seem strange that banks which had just received more than a thousand million dollars from the government should not have been able to increase the money supply in the hands of the public without damage to themselves, by expanding their own loans to customers, or at least by cashing checks presented by their depositors. Subsequent inquiry discovered that the loans from the RFC tied up the best and safest collateral still in the hands of the banks, leaving little to back an enlargement of loans to the public. The banks were in no condition to borrow from any source. After the Franklin Roosevelt administration acceded to office, the mistake was rectified by substituting, for loans from the RFC, investment in banks' preferred stock, which tied up no collateral but instead expanded the banks' resources.

The International Crisis

Before the policy of artificially sustaining capital values developed, however, attention was distracted from the domestic muddle by dramatic events abroad. By 1931 depression was smashing the intrinsically weak and crazy structure of international trade and finance. Nations, no one of which could produce all that it consumed or consume all that it produced, had been trying to act as if they were independent economic units. Following the example set by the United States Congress when it passed the Smoot-Hawley Tariff Act, they were raising trade barriers against one another and thus deepening the crisis of all. When the flow of international credits dried up, the inconsistency of the existing debt framework was revealed: Germany, for instance, which had built up its entire economic structure on the basis of an excess of imports over exports, and had before the war paid for this excess by the earnings on its foreign investments and shipping services, now had to pay foreigners the interest on the debt it had accumulated after the war, not to speak of reparation. The fall of prices made all debt payments more difficult, even aside from the drop in the physical volume of trade.

It was necessary to knock over only one financial domino in order to upset the whole row. Germany, in her extremity, tried to establish a customs union with Austria and thus beat down at least one wall of the barrier about her. France became frightened at the political implications of this approach to "Anschluss" and vetoed it. Directly or indirectly, French financial interests, which had been extending help to Austria, caused the withdrawal of credits from her, and the first domino went over with the collapse of the Creditanstalt. German financial institutions, which were also involved in Austria, were already weak enough so that this endangered them; a bank holiday ensued in Germany. London, which had been sending short-term credit to Germany to earn the high rates of interest there, thus became involved. The British credits were frozen. The French and others who had large liquid funds in England withdrew them rapidly. Thus gold flowed out from London in immense quantities. A Labour government in Britain was overthrown by a bitter attack, on the basis that its domestic spending endangered the gold standard. The National government that succeeded it was promptly forced off the gold standard by the sudden excess of outgoing payments over incoming ones. Controls were established over German exchange, to hold Germany's gold reserves at the expense of foreign trade and payments. The exchange value of the pound sterling, unlinked from gold, fell. Other countries closely dependent on British trade promptly followed Britain off gold.

If anything was to be saved out of this confusion, the first step was obviously to get rid of the burden of political debts—reparations and war-debt payments. The main source of political payments was Germany: she owed reparations principally to France and England; France owed war debts mainly to England and in much smaller measure to the United States; England owed war debts to us. We were, according to contract, the ultimate recipients of the flow. It was therefore up to us to move first. After much pressure, and too late to prevent most of the damage, President Hoover suggested a moratorium on war debts and reparations, and the suggestion was accepted. At Lausanne the recipients of reparations agreed virtually to their cancellation, expecting that war debts would be canceled in turn. The Lausanne meeting was regarded at the time as setting the course for further action to clear up the tangle of trade barriers, private debts, and currency instability.

These events abroad prevented any prompt improvement of business through a revival of exports. To say this is not, of course, to say that revival would have come if the row of financial dominoes had not fallen and the gold standard had not been weakened. Entirely aside from the additional restrictions on trade produced by the financial crisis, each capitalist nation had long been striving to increase its exports without increasing its imports, and the inevitable result of this policy on world markets is a surplus of goods for sale, falling prices, and depression. There can be no market where everyone wants to sell and no one wants to buy. The United States had been a chief offender in this respect. It therefore came with bad grace from our administration to blame the rest of the world for our failure to recover. This ignored the effect of our policy upon the rest of the world. It also ignored the immense obstacles to recovery in the internal economy of the United States itself, and within each of the other nations concerned. To say that the depression was international, though true enough, was only a convenient alibi for each national government. Depressions do not occur in the middle of the Atlantic and Pacific oceans, or solely along international boundaries.

What really had happened was that the international gold standard and the international debt structure had broken under the strain of continued depression. Their breaking was not an accident; if it had not come about in this precise way, it would have come about in some other. And the nations which left gold, being thereby placed in a somewhat more advantageous competitive position with regard to exports, were subsequently able to moderate a little the full force of the depression within their borders. Their gain was others' loss in the shrinking world markets, and to that extent the United States was injured. But neither the gain nor the loss was great; the volume of world trade had become so small in any event that shifts in its sharing were of relatively little consequence. British prices ceased falling rapidly, but British trade hardly increased. If Britain had never left the gold standard, we still could not have sold abroad much greater quantities of wheat or cotton or automobiles or agricultural machinery.

Why Credit Failed to Expand

Two more devices of Hoover planning remain to be discussed briefly. One was work-sharing. This was, in reality, unemployment-sharing. It had no influence whatever on the amount of work to be done. It meant merely that the work—and the pay for it—should be distributed more evenly. It meant giving jobs at extremely low wages to some of the unemployed, at the expense of the wages of the employed. It transferred some of the burden from the shoulders of those who were giving charity to the shoulders of workers who were less able to pay for it.

The other was the effort to stimulate business by an easy credit policy. Interest rates had been kept low ever since the beginning of the depression, but credit obstinately refused to expand. The Federal Reserve Banks began to buy government bonds. In this way they accumulated about $500 million of excess reserves. It has been shown that in prosperous times such action, by increasing the liquid assets of member banks, tends to stimulate more lending. If the member banks sell the bonds to the Federal Reserve, they thereby accumulate funds. Private persons who sell bonds presumably deposit the proceeds. Thus the banks receive large amounts of money, either currency or "bank money"—i.e., deposits on their books—which is not earning any interest. The theory was that they would be forced to lend this money in order that it might earn something. An expansion of reserves in the Federal Reserve Banks can, under ordinary circumstances, lead to an expansion of lending by the member banks about ten times as large as the growth of reserves. This was thought to be an easy and simple way of enlarging the amount of purchasing power in circulation. It was a moderate type of inflation.

But it did not work. The ordinary capitalist machinery failed here as it had elsewhere. The people who needed the money, and who would have to start buying if the rest of the business machine were to operate, could not borrow from the banks. Wage-earners of course could not borrow; farmers could not. Businessmen who were already weighted down by debts and had shrinking markets were not good risks. Banks are accustomed to lend only to concerns which have business prospects. It is one thing to believe that, if the banks would simultaneously expand loans to the whole business community, all would begin to buy more and everybody would have better prospects. It is another to expect individual banks to start the process by lending to individual customers at the bottom of a depression, without being assured that all the other banks were going to do the same thing and thus that all loans would be made more safe. Banks, though part of a system which, on account of its close interrelationship, requires collective action, do not act collectively, because they are privately owned, profit-seeking enterprises. The proponents of the credit-expansion cure were thinking of the banks as if they were a single system, a social instrument.

Furthermore, the banks were afraid even to take risks that normally they would regard as good. A large part of their assets had become frozen in real-estate loans, in bonds and stocks that had shrunk amazingly in value. To attempt to turn these assets into cash at the prevailing prices would bring certain disaster. The always considerable number of bank failures was growing. Nobody knew when depositors in large numbers might begin withdrawals. The instinct of self-preservation therefore led banks to keep as liquid as possible. They took advantage of the Federal Reserve policy, first to reduce their indebtedness to the Reserve Banks, second to accumulate cash. The banks were themselves the first and largest hoarders. The self-preservative action on the part of individual banks had the same result as the effort on the part of each business to throw depression losses on others. It deepened the depression and made the situation more dangerous for all. Rapidly the banks slid toward the crisis of March 1933. The more they apprehended the calamity, the more they did to make certain its arrival.

Hoover was reported to be very angry at the banks for their failure to expand loans and so to stimulate recovery. In this he reflected the unpopularity of the banks among mortgagors who had been foreclosed or threatened with foreclosure, among borrowers on collateral who had been sold out, among depositors who had lost their money by failures, among businessmen and farmers who could not borrow to meet current obligations. The "international" bankers were unpopular because of the collapse of foreign ventures, the investment bankers because of the loss to investors in security issues. All this irritation was given point by the beginning of a long series of revelations concerning prominent bankers who had served their own interests by shady practices at the expense of the public; thus a split appeared in the citadel of capitalism itself. Logically, however, neither the President nor the other objectors had a very good case. The bankers were merely acting on the prescriptions of rugged individualism. Comparatively little of the trouble was caused by outright dishonesty. We cannot expect one section of the community to act collectively for the general good when other sections do not do so, when it is not organized to do so, and when all have been nourished on the principle that if each unit acts in its own interest the interest of all will be served.

And so the closing months of the Hoover administration saw a complete rout of everything he had tried to do, because he had followed the prescriptions of the ruling groups themselves, and these prescriptions led to illogical and unworkable policies. At the beginning, businessmen could not effectively cooperate to maintain the status quo, since that status was impossible to maintain. Confidence could not be restored by optimistic statements, because more than confidence was lacking. A policy of governmental non-interference permitting deflation to work through to its logical end could not be carried out because capitalism itself would not permit deflation of the most rigid elements in the structure, which needed deflation the most. Contradictory international policies which had long been followed caused an international crisis which interposed a further obstacle to recovery; belated and partial action was ineffective; the reparations and debt moratorium merely held the crisis in solution. And the effort to stimulate credit expansion by the banks was mired in the dismal swamp of financial individualism. Hoarding increased and gold withdrawals swelled. Michigan and then other whole states declared banking holidays in order to save what reserves they had and throw the burden elsewhere. The burden of withdrawals, not only for hoarding but to carry on current business, rapidly became concentrated on New York, and by the last days of February 1933, which were also the last days of Hoover's term in office, the whole banking complex was tottering. Panic was on.

CHAPTER 9

The First New Deal

Franklin D. Roosevelt, who became President in March 1933, was neither a student of economics nor an adherent of any comprehensive program for altering the economic system. He had never run a business or carried on a learned profession; he did not need to earn his living. He could, and did, dedicate himself to the career of a public servant. In that capacity he had learned how to enlist the advice of experts in social and economic problems. As Governor of the State of New York he had become accustomed to this practice. He liked people, and they liked him. He had compassion for the unfortunate and worked harmoniously with leaders in social services. Above all, he was a superb politician, in the best sense of the word. By long experience he had learned when and how to achieve his aims in dealing with lawmakers and other political professionals.

In preparing himself for the campaign, Roosevelt began to gather experts, later popularly known as "Brain Trusters." Prominent among them were Rexford Guy Tugwell and Raymond Moley of the Columbia University faculty; Henry Wallace, a leader of reform in agriculture; Herbert Feis, Adolph Berle, and Donald Richberg, three experts in public law and economic problems. These and many others who were called to Washington did not comprise a closely bound unit; they often disagreed, but each was competent in his specialty. The President listened to them, chose what to do next, and decided how to do it. He described himself as a quarterback in a football game, calling signals; if one play did not suffice, he would try another.

The state of the nation when Roosevelt assumed the Presidency required rescue missions. The banking system had to be saved from shipwreck. The farmers had to be guarded against bankruptcy. The unemployed had to be fed, clothed, and housed. Expert advisers told him what he could do in each concrete problem; he knew how to explain his program in each case, telling the people what he favored, and why. Congress acted quickly under his leadership, largely because action was urgent and because the people supported the President. In the end, some piecemeal economic planning had been done, and some important modifications of the economic order had been gained. But the main achievement of Franklin D. Roosevelt in his first term was the rescue of the capitalist order from its own mistakes, not the permanent establishment of a new system of central economic planning.

In addition to the emergency measures, however, the New Dealers did, during the President's first term, create three new agencies which they hoped would be permanent and which were designed to introduce basic changes by use of economic planning. These were the Agricultural Adjustment Administration (May 12, 1933), the Tennessee Valley Authority (May 18, 1933), and the National Industrial Recovery Act (June 16, 1933). The Supreme Court in 1936 held unconstitutional parts of the AAA and in 1935 demolished most of the NIRA. Only the TVA survived in its original form. The construction of dams, lakes, and electrical works required so long a time that much of the work was actually done in Roosevelt's second term of office; it will be discussed in Chapter 10.

Saving the Banks

On March 4, 1933, when President Roosevelt was inaugurated, the cornerstone of any modern economy, capitalist or socialist, had crumbled. Banks, the chief sources of money, had either closed their doors or were about to do so within a few hours. In his inaugural address the new President promised quick and efficient action. On March 6 he issued an order legally suspending all banking functions, and he declared that no bank would be reopened if it was not in good condition. In order to safeguard the gold reserves, he forbade the export of gold and directed banks not to pay out gold in exchange for currency. On March 7 bank members of the Federal Reserve System were ordered to deliver to the Reserve Banks all their gold or gold certificates. On March 9 Congress passed an Emergency Banking Act which endorsed the actions taken by the President. It also authorized the Reconstruction Finance Corporation (which previously had been lending to banks in such a way that they could not enlarge the money supply in the hands of their customers) to buy banks' preferred stock and so to improve their condition by enlarging their unpledged resources.

On March 12 President Roosevelt gave his first Fireside Chat over the radio networks. He explained, in terms that everybody could understand, what he had done about the banks. He assured his listeners that banks which reopened for business would be safe. The talk transmuted into confidence the nationwide money panic. By March 15—three days after the fireside chat—half of the banks, possessing nine-tenths of the banking resources, had been reopened. Within three weeks more than a billion dollars of currency withdrawn by the banks' customers was redeposited. By April 5 individual depositors, required to return to the banks all gold and gold certificates they had withdrawn, had deposited $50 million more in gold than they had taken from the banks since January 1, 1933.

Some banks were controlled by federal agents while their affairs were put in order, but in the end only 5 per cent were permanently closed. And Congress minimized future runs on banks by legislation which insured deposits up to $10,000 per depositor. It would be difficult to imagine a better tonic for popular confidence in the new President than this course of action.

Budget and Federal Expenditure

A curious incident in the "first hundred days" of the New Deal, during which the President and Congress outdid all previous records of legislation, was an attempt to balance the federal budget.

This effort illustrates the variety of opinion among Mr. Roosevelt's advisers and the absence in his own mind of any coherent economic theory or scheme of planning.

During the campaign he had promised to reduce federal expenditure by 25 per cent and to balance the budget—as his opponent, President Hoover, wished to do. Lewis Douglas, Roosevelt's Budget Director, strongly urged that policy. On March 20, 1933, Congress passed the Economy Act, pledging to hold down federal expenditures and even cutting salaries of federal employees by 10 per cent. Yet almost immediately thereafter the President proposed, and Congress sanctioned, large appropriations for unemployment relief and other expensive projects. To stimulate economic recovery required massive governmental spending. A balanced federal budget could not be achieved until after prosperity had returned.

Before the end of March, the first month of the new administration, Congress authorized the establishment of a Civilian Conservation Corps, one of the more successful New Deal agencies. It put to work on forestry and other public improvements young men who volunteered; they earned weekly wages which were sent to unemployed parents; they were well fed and clothed, and they received education appropriate to their ages. By the end of July 300,000 young men were established in 1300 camps and were engaged in various conservation projects.

On May 12 Congress established the Federal Emergency Relief Administration and provided funds to sustain the adult unemployed. FERA was the first of a series of such administrations. It offered grants to public relief agencies of states and local governments; soon about 4 million families were on relief, at a cost to the federal government of some $150 million a month. On November 8, 1933, Congress passed a new measure to aid the unemployed more directly and with less injury to their self-respect —the Civil Works Administration, which soon put to work more than 4 million persons improving public property, and thus in less than two years spent nearly $1 billion. Experience with this type of unemployment compensation led to a more imaginative and effective measure in 1935, the WPA (Works Progress Administra-

tion). It turned back the "unemployables" to state and local
agencies and put the others to work in their customary occupations—including trades, professions, and literary or artistic work.
More than 250,000 projects were financed; the compensation was
small, but larger than in previous forms of relief. Between August
1935 and 1941, when preparation for war virtually eliminated unemployment, WPA included more than 2 million workers a year
and paid them, in the six years, $11,365 million.

On May 12 Congress had passed the Agricultural Adjustment
Act, which would require large governmental funds, and on May
18 it established the Tennessee Valley Authority, which, although
it would eventually earn enough to pay its expenses, could not
construct great dams, generating stations, and power lines without large appropriations. Still another obligation was undertaken
by passage of the Emergency Farm Mortgage Act, to save bank-
rupt farmers' land by refinancing mortgages. And on June 13 a
similar protection was offered to home-owners by the Home-
Owners' Loan Act.

More Governmental Regulation

While the federal government began rescue work for the unemployed and the farmers, the President and Congress did not overlook the need for measures to prevent fraud or weakness in the
financial markets. On May 27, 1933, the Truth in Securities Act
became law, establishing the Securities and Exchange Commission. This law sought to prevent the recurrence of former abuses
by requiring that all business concerns which offered for sale their
bonds and stocks must publish financial reports, according to requirements specified by the commission. The commission also
was given power to oversee, and if necessary to regulate, the practices of professional dealers in the stock exchange or other financial markets. Other duties of the commission included the dissolu-
tion of utility holding companies which were more than one degree removed from the operating companies or had no logical
function arising from concentration in a given area, and the supervision of any new security issued or any acquisition of property
by interstate utility companies. The Federal Power Commission

was directed by the law to regulate rates and service of the interstate power companies. The utility companies concerned fought a
bitter war against the new legislation, by delay and litigation, but in
the end had to surrender.

The Glass-Steagall Act, which became law on June 16, required that thereafter commercial banks could not own or be af-
filiated with investment banks, whose business was to sell securities. Thus, a commercial bank could no longer use its depositors' money to buy securities offered for sale by an affiliate of
the bank—a practice involving a conflict of interest, since the commercial bank would be buying with one hand what it sold with
the other. This rigorous reform compelled even the old and leading
J. P. Morgan and Company to separate its strictly banking services
from flotation of new issues of securities.

On the same day Congress passed the Railroad Coordination
Act in an effort to increase the efficiency of the carriers, a task
formerly attempted in vain by the ill-fated Transportation Act of
1920. The railroads were among the chief sufferers from the depression, and many of them were being subsidized by the Reconstruction Finance Corporation. Increases in their rates would
serve principally to drive away traffic to their competitors—truck
and automobile transport, airlines, pipelines, and water carriers.
An experienced member of the Interstate Commerce Commission, Joseph B. Eastman, was appointed Railroad Coordinator.
The best he could do was not enough; he had no executive power.
At every turn he had to negotiate with the private administrators
of the several railroad companies, many of whom had been more
concerned with dealing in railroad securities and promoting holding
companies than with providing efficient operation of the lines.
And the railroads, even with the best management, could not have
avoided operating losses until recovery of the national economy
enlarged their traffic.

Monetary Change

Almost all the measures so far discussed in this chapter were designed for the emergency; on a national scale they corresponded
to public assistance for victims of hurricanes, floods, or earth-

quakes. They aimed in a general way to rescue the economy from nationwide calamity or, in a few instances, to prevent in the future certain specific abuses. They remind one also of the task of a housekeeper making repairs and sweeping away dust and dirt.

There remain several undertakings of the New Deal which were designed not merely to aid the needy or stimulate recovery, but to alter the institutions which had failed to prevent calamity, or to introduce new and, it was hoped, more wholesome policies. Some succeeded; others did not.

In the United States, long before the great depression of the 1930s, there had been many controversies about monetary policy. Some wanted currency based on both gold and silver, others wanted the gold standard alone. Some even favored "fiat money" based on nothing but governmental issue—like the greenbacks of the Civil War. Eventually, at the turn of the century, the United States had adopted the gold standard, in the sense that anyone possessing lawful paper currency could exchange it at par value for gold or gold certificates. Exceptions could be made in the form of dollar bills or two-dollar bills representing silver. The principal argument for this (modified) gold standard was that it would prevent inflation, since the total amount of money would be limited by the stock of gold—everywhere accepted as having high intrinsic worth. When the Federal Reserve System was organized, the law provided that the gold reserve must be at least enough to cover 40 per cent of the currency in circulation, and at the same time cover 35 per cent of deposit accounts.

In the depression of the 1930s there was obviously no inflationary rise of prices; prices were falling. Anyone who had an income could buy more cheaply than before, but incomes were shrinking, and millions of persons had no earnings at all. Yet some politicians and even a few economists thought that the cause of the economic collapse was an insufficient quantity of money, tied as it was to the nation's stock of gold. The old controversy was revived.

The President had managed to mobilize the gold reserve by telling citizens to deposit gold in their possession—much of which they had recently withdrawn from the banks—by ordering the banks to deposit their gold in the Reserve Banks, and by requiring the Reserve Banks to turn the gold over to the United States Treasury, accepting gold certificates in return. Thus the banks would again be free to increase paper currency in circulation and expand loans to the public without exceeding the maximum legal ratios between gold on the one hand and outstanding money on the other. Whatever the monetary expansionists might think, the gold standard was not limiting the amount of money in the hands of the public. Only if the nation could restore full employment and business prosperity could there be any possible danger that the gold standard would retard economic growth.

Some who had the ear of the President, however, urged a change which, without abandoning the gold standard altogether, would permit a larger limit to the expansion of money of all sorts by "reducing the gold content of the dollar." But within the United States the actual ratios between the existing gold reserve and the outstanding currency and deposits were nowhere near the limit established by existing law, and so changing the legal gold content of the dollar would not enlarge the amount of dollars in possession of the public.

In international transactions, however, reducing the gold content of the dollar would have an immediate effect. Almost all trading nations were on a gold standard. The units of the currency of each were equivalent to some statutory weight of monetary gold. If the United States, for example, decreed that hereafter the value of the dollar would equal only half as much weight in gold as before, and the British retained the old gold value of the pound, prices of American goods exported would be, in British money, only half as much as before, whereas British goods imported by the United States would cost twice as many dollars as previously. Devaluation of the currency unit was therefore a means of creating a handicap in international trade against producers and exporters in countries which did not devalue. Some economists called this policy "beggar thy neighbor." During the early years of the world-wide depression numerous nations did devalue, thus inducing devaluation by trading partners. This merry-go-round, as it was often called, introduced chaotic conditions in international trade; in the end nobody could benefit from it.

During his first week in office President Roosevelt forbade the export of monetary gold; on April 20 this instruction was altered to permit no export of gold without the consent of the United States Treasury. (International balance of payments could not be maintained unless shipments of gold out of, or into, a nation covered the difference between incoming and outgoing value of international transactions.)

On June 5 Congress reflected the intention of many of its members to clear the way for abandonment of the gold standard, by making invalid the gold clause in contracts. Many contracts had included this clause, which bound the payer to meet his obligation with gold, if so required by the payee. Though infrequently invoked, this gold clause was supposed to assure the payee by diminishing his risk. The act of Congress gave rise to litigation on constitutional grounds, yet the Supreme Court validated it in 1935.

In June and July 1933 an international conference in London attempted to end the competition in devaluing exchange rates, which in the long run would benefit nobody. The United States was represented in the conference. The President, contrary to the judgment of his envoys, torpedoed the whole effort in order to keep a free hand in valuing United States money. And on January 31, 1934, Roosevelt, by the permission of Congress, devalued the dollar, reducing its "gold content" by about 40 per cent. This action did little to stop the decline of incomes or expand exports and limit imports. The basic trouble in the United States was a matter of incomes, not of the value of money, and before long the nations with which the United States traded were compelled to reduce the gold values of their own currencies. Our Presidential quarterback, having met failure in this play, turned to other means of advancing the football.

Planning for Farmers

The Farm Board under Mr. Hoover's administration had failed to increase farm incomes because it did not succeed in its aim of limiting crops in order to raise their prices. The government stored ever-growing hoards of grain and cotton with a loss of about $150 million; these surpluses hung over the market. The New Deal attacked the problem with new devices, embodied in the Agricultural Adjustment Act of May 1933.

In the cases of most field crops, the Agricultural Adjustment Administration (AAA) attempted to limit the output by decreasing the acreages planted. By an ingenious scheme known as the Domestic Allotment Plan, each farmer was told by how many acres he would be expected to diminish the planting of each crop. First the agricultural statisticians calculated by what percentage the national total of each crop must be reduced in order to raise the price to the desired amount. This total was broken down by states, counties, and individual farms, so that each farmer would know how many acres he was expected to hold out of production. The plan would be put into effect only if a majority of the growers voted for it. If a majority did consent, any individual farmer could still refuse to sign the agreement, but in that case he would deprive himself of the subsidy that was to be paid to the signers.

In the case of cotton-growers, a somewhat different incentive was applied. If a majority agreed to reduce the planted acreage by the amount expected to raise selling prices, each participant would have the option of purchasing at the lower prices, from the governmental stores in warehouses, as much cotton as he agreed not to raise. If the plan succeeded in increasing the price, he could sell this stored cotton at a profit. If it did not succeed, the farmers need not exercise their options. The money to finance this indirect subsidy was provided by a processing tax imposed on the mills or other processors of the crops.

By 1934 plans to increase selling prices had been applied to cotton, wheat, corn, hogs, tobacco, cattle, peanuts, sugar beets, sugar cane, and potatoes. In 1936, however, a conservative Supreme Court invalidated the agreements to restrict acreage and the processing tax. The administration softened the blow to the farmers by subsidizing their participation in a program to prevent soil erosion and improve its fertility.

In 1938 Congress passed a new Agricultural Adjustment Act,

omitting the processing tax. In other respects it was much like the original law. It did embody, however, a concept named by Secretary of Agriculture Wallace "the ever normal granary." Surplus crops, above the amount required to maintain the price decided upon, could be stored. The grower, using his warehouse receipts as security, could borrow from a governmentally owned Commodity Credit Corporation, at the price expected by the AAA to be attained by crop restriction. If this price was achieved, the farmer could sell the produce and repay his loan. If prices were lower than this, the farmer could retain the money he had borrowed; the Commodity Credit Corporation would destroy his note. Thus a bounteous crop could be in part withheld from the markets, whereas a poor crop could be augmented by release of grain, cotton, or other farm products in storage.

The President, who in 1936 had been re-elected by the largest majority on record (he lost only Maine and Vermont), appointed several new and more liberal justices of the Supreme Court as older members of the court retired. The new AAA was not declared unconstitutional. Yet the stores in government warehouses kept growing; there were no really lean years. The government reduced the oversupply by selling foodstuffs in foreign nations at prices lower than those at home, by using them for school lunches, and by other devices. Farmers, though limited in planted acres, often increased their output per acre by planting the more fertile fields or by better cultivation. Insofar as output was limited, the cause was largely bad weather conditions, particularly dust storms in the arid Southwest.

The record shows that agricultural output in the nation declined 6 per cent between 1932 and 1936, but thereafter increased again. The principal goal of the whole gigantic operation—to raise the prices farmers received as much as the prices farmers had to pay, using the years just before World War I as the base—would have succeeded if the "parity index" had reached 100. This index, which was only 55 in 1932, did rise to 92 in 1937. It did not reach 100 before World War II. The gain may have been partly due to the planned restriction of agricultural output, but a major influence was the rise in the purchasing power of consumers, stimulated as it was by a partial recovery from the depths of the depression and by governmental aids to the unemployed.

Planning for Industry

On June 16, 1933, Congress authorized planning in the interest of industry, of a sort resembling proposals advocated by spokesmen for employers, combined with proposals advocated by labor leaders, and also with the program of increasing public works in order to provide a stimulus to economic recovery.

Private industry wanted an end to "cutthroat competition," one reason for the downward drift of prices. Consequently Title I of the National Industrial Recovery Act suspended the antitrust laws, so that in each industry the employers could agree on a "code of fair practice" outlawing price competition, if approved by a representative of the federal government. By implication, this clause legalized agreements to limit output in the interest of higher prices.

Each code, to satisfy labor, was supposed to set minimum wages and maximum hours of work. And Section 7A guaranteed to labor the right of collective bargaining.

Title II of NIRA sought to stimulate public construction, in order to increase earnings of the population by governmental deficit-spending. Secretary of the Interior Harold Ickes administered this section of the law.

To supervise the operation of Title I, a National Recovery Administration was created. The Administrator, General Hugh Johnson, had worked with Bernard M. Baruch during World War I in the War Industries Board. Deputy administrators under him had the right to sanction or disapprove of codes. Each deputy was expected to have advisers representing industry, labor, and consumers.

The passage of this law stimulated production before many codes were adopted. Manufacturers expected higher selling prices; their costs had not yet risen by agreements with labor or by application of minimum wages and maximum hours. Factory output increased by nearly 50 per cent; payrolls grew by only half that amount. Obviously industry could make larger profits by failing to adopt codes than by adopting them.

To end this private exploitation of delay, the President issued a Re-employment Agreement in July 1933. He asked business firms to employ no children under 16, and to pay minimum wages of 40 cents an hour or more for a maximum work-week of 35 hours. Every employer signing the agreement could display a "blue eagle" emblem supplied by the government and was entitled to use the slogan "We do our part"; purchasers were asked to boycott firms who failed to sign. More than 2 million firms did sign; the consequent rise in labor costs stimulated the drafting and acceptance of codes, which in turn would raise prices also.

During its lifetime—ended on May 27, 1935, by a Supreme Court decision that Title I of the law was unconstitutional—557 codes were approved. Only 3 of the codes authorized consumer representatives; only 37 code authorities contained representatives of labor with voting rights.

Most of the New Deal "Brain Trusters" were not sorry that the experiment had to be abandoned. Privately owned industries had been given the task of national planning, with the cooperation of labor and consumers, in the interest of the national economy. For the most part they ignored their employees and customers, increased prices, and sought profits as if each industry were a monopoly. The law meant to them a license to discipline competitors who reduced prices below those stipulated in the codes. It is not strange that a majority of the Supreme Court justices ruled Title I of the law unconstitutional, largely on the ground that under it the federal government had delegated duties which only it had the right to perform.

A few, such as Rexford Guy Tugwell, thought the mistake was not in the plan of NRA but in its administration. Arthur M. Schlesinger, Jr., in *The Politics of Upheaval*, describes Tugwell's conversation with the President about the subject.

In September 1934 Roosevelt had asked Tugwell to come to Hyde Park for the Labor Day weekend to go over the NRA problem. They chatted in Roosevelt's bedroom before church on Sunday morning, the President in an old sweater amidst a clutter of Sunday papers, fitting one cigarette after another into his long holder as he talked. His doubts were plain enough. Did not the NRA experience show that the nation was not yet ready to function as an integrated economy on the basis of national planning? The trouble, Tugwell replied, was not in the idea, but in the execution. Roosevelt reminded him that he himself had approved of Johnson as administrator. Yes, yes, this turned out to be wrong; but the fact that the experiment had gone badly this time did not prove that it would never succeed. Tugwell begged for an extension of NRA, suggesting that Johnson be replaced by a board. Roosevelt seemed to agree. . . . As the car came up to the church door, Tugwell had a sudden perception that he had failed. . . . "I was asking too much. It was not only NRA, it was the whole organic conception of the living nation, equipped with institutions for foresight, conjecture, and balance. It was not yet time for it. . . . I knew that NRA was done for; and I hardly expected to see another attempt of the sort in my lifetime."

Title II of the law, supposed to increase public construction, seemed slow to spur action. Secretary of the Interior Harold Ickes had to supervise the drafting of plans, approve contracts, and create the necessary administrative agency. His critics charged that his emphasis on preventing political graft unnecessarily delayed the projects. The total value of public construction at its previous high point, 1930, was $2858 million. Its lowest total during the depression, 1933, was only $1648 million. Between that year, when NIRA became law, and 1935, when Title I of the act was ruled unconstitutional, the value of public construction had risen to $2233 million, or by nearly one-third. To the extent that this gain reflected activity under Title II of the Recovery Act, "Honest Harold" probably contributed more to economic recovery than the whole complex machinery of industrial codes, especially since the life of the NRA infant lasted only two years, whereas public construction could continue indefinitely; it was unquestionably constitutional.

CHAPTER 10

The Second New Deal

In one sense the first New Deal consisted of the activities of the federal government during Franklin D. Roosevelt's first term in office (1933-1937), while the second New Deal was the sum of the policies adopted between 1937 and 1941. But the difference between the first and the second was more than the mere passage of time. The effort of the first New Deal to enforce economic planning in industry and agriculture, somewhat in the style of Soviet Russian (or, as many said, of Italian Fascist) planning, was made impossible by the Supreme Court when it ruled that NIRA and AAA were in part unconstitutional. The second New Deal approached planning of the national economy from a different direction. It paid more attention to the volume of money and credit and began to understand the uses of deficit spending on the part of government. It also turned its attention to the need for regulating big business, especially the public services, and to improving the status of labor and the retired by means of unemployment insurance and social security. If the first New Deal was that of the planners, or Brain Trusters, the second was more properly that of the spenders and regulators.

That is the general picture, in the perspective of many years, but it was confused at the time by conflicts within the Roosevelt administration. One doctrine held by many of the President's supporters distrusted bigness in both business and government. Justice Brandeis of the Supreme Court was an intellectual leader of this doctrine. It emphasized the importance of the individual and the local government and held—as Brandeis maintained—that the trouble in our economy was not competitive laissez faire but rather the stifling of free competition by big business itself. In many respects the Brandeis school was in the tradition of Woodrow Wilson's New Freedom. Its adherents supported the "death sentence" for utility holding companies decreed under the first New Deal. They favored better living standards for labor and the measures that offered aid to the unemployed. Unemployment insurance they regarded with favor, although they preferred to have it administered by the several states. Except for central planning of the NRA type, they felt that most reforms of the first New Deal should be carried through.

Most of these reforms, adopted as an aid to recovery, demanded large spending by the federal government. Such spending could not be met by tax revenue as long as the depression lasted. Most New Dealers, including those of the Brandeis school, strongly favored the reforms even though they required a continuing unbalanced budget. Some, however, like Secretary of the Treasury Morgenthau, wanted to defer the reforms until the budget was balanced. Roosevelt himself inclined now to one side of the argument and now to the other. He supported the Economy Act of March 20, 1933, intended to reduce government spending, but he also strongly supported subsequent legislation appropriating large funds to help the unemployed. This he did because of his humanity, regardless of any theory. What the New Deal needed was a respectable economic theory that would sanction large governmental expenditure even if it exceeded income from taxes.

Keynesian Economics

That theory was supplied by a brilliant British economist connected with Cambridge University, John Maynard Keynes. He had previously attracted attention by his *Economic Consequences of the Peace* (1919), which deplored the Treaty of Versailles for its economic fragmentation of Europe and its unlimited penalty of reparations imposed on Germany. The book was a best-seller in the years immediately after World War I, in the United States as well as in Britain.

Now Keynes developed a new body of economic principles concerning the policies to be followed in order to prevent unemployment and stimulate economic growth. He prepared a program for the British Liberal Party in the 1929 election, recommending an expansion of governmental construction. In 1930 he published *A Treatise on Money*, a highly technical volume expounding his views. There, as in other publications, he argued that the best way for government to stimulate production and employment is to spend more money than it receives in taxes.

Felix Frankfurter (later to become a Justice of the Supreme Court) met Keynes in England. He gave him a note of introduction to the President when Keynes later came to the United States to receive an honorary degree from Columbia University. Mr. Roosevelt invited him to tea at the White House on May 28, 1934, and the two met on other occasions. But the President was not a scholar in economic theory, and though he said that he enjoyed the interviews he later remarked to Secretary of Labor Frances Perkins, "He left a whole rigmarole of figures. He must be a mathematician rather than a political economist." And Keynes said to Miss Perkins that he had supposed the President was "more literate, economically speaking."

In 1936 Keynes's major work on the subject was published, *The General Theory of Employment, Interest and Money*. Like his *Treatise on Money*, it is not easy reading for the layman, but its main conclusions may be roughly summarized. He began his great book with an adroit introduction. The classical economic doctrines were logical enough, he said, but they could hold true only in a special case—the case limited by many assumptions, not the actual situation. He proposed to develop a general theory for which unrealistic assumptions would not be required.

Every payment, he said, has two sides. The recipient receives as much as the payer spends—just that and no more. Income flows in a circle about the economic system. If there is a fall in general demand, it must be due to a shrinkage in the flow of income. One must look for the cause of the shrinkage; who is holding money out of the stream?

Clearly, money spent by consumers (and everybody is a consumer) is not withheld from spending. Any money withheld by them, at least temporarily, is what people save. The economic classicists assumed that all savings are invested and so necessarily expended by business. Keynes challenged this assumption. The savers are frequently not the same people as the investors, and have different motives. You and I deposit money in a bank or pay it to an insurance company; the money is not spent unless someone uses it to put up houses or enlarge a business.

In respect to the national economy, Keynes argued that if a government spends money only to the extent of its receipts from taxation, it does not increase the national income. But government can increase that income, he pointed out, and stimulate employment by spending more than it receives in taxes. The enlargement of production and national income so achieved is financed by the issuance of government bonds, or by borrowing in some other way from the banks, just as private business may enlarge its output and employ more workers by means of bank loans or the issuance of securities.

What Brought Recovery?

All the specific measures under the New Deal depended for their ultimate success on increased incomes and spending by the people. The record shows that the Gross National Product or Expenditure —which means all spending by final users—increased from $61.5 billion in 1933, the lowest point in the depression, to $91.3 billion in 1939, the last year not affected by World War II. These totals are modified to cancel all changes in prices: the dollar so modified was in 1933 equal in purchasing power to the dollar in 1939. Thus the real expenditure of the people increased by about 50 per cent in these six years.

How did the consumers get the money? Spending by the federal, state, and local governments (also in terms of 1939 dollars) increased from $8.7 billion in 1933 to $13.1 billion in 1939. Gross investment by private business rose (in 1939 dollars) from $1.6 billion in 1933 to $8.3 billion in 1939. In both cases, the money spent by government or invested by private business was derived largely from borrowing, and most of the borrowed money came, ultimately, from the banking system, as had the borrowing incident to World War I. Governmental deficits ranged between a low of $1.4 billion in 1933 and a high of $3 billion in 1936. In the years between 1933, when the New Deal began, and 1939 (inclusive), 1938 was an exception, to be examined presently. The Keynes formula had in effect been practiced by the New Deal ever since the Democrats came to power; the new economic theory justified this means of recovery and persuaded the administration that it was largely responsible for gains already made and should be the major instrument in the future.

Governments may spend without expecting profit as a consequence of the investment, and they can spend more money than they receive in taxes, by borrowing. If a newly issued government bond is bought by a hoarder of savings, it puts that idle sum into circulation. And if a government bond is bought by a purchaser who borrows the money from a bank, that much money joins the stream of income. Government expenditure is as good as private investment in stimulating the economy. And if a government has a budget surplus, it is taking more from the citizens than it pays out.

Economists and others among the "Brain Trusters" met and talked with Keynes during his visits to this country. Academic economists did not have to wait for his *General Theory* in 1936 in order to understand his main theme and act accordingly. Professor Alvin Hansen of Minnesota (later of Harvard) received a copy of the Keynes manuscript before its publication and reported its contents to a conference on a weekend in the Berkshires in Massachusetts. Two graduate students at the Yale Law School who had studied with Keynes at Cambridge led a seminar on his views in the early 1930s. Several faculty members of the Yale Law School later became advisers to the President; some were appointed to important offices.

Partly because of the influence of Keynesian economists, the government building program did not cease when the National Industrial Recovery Act was canceled. It had authorized "low-rent and slum-clearance projects"; the Public Works Administration had set up a Housing Division. Local dividend-limited companies were ready to receive federal grants. Under state laws, some fifty public housing authorities had been created. In

1937 the Wagner-Steagall Act substituted for the PWA agency a United States Housing Authority in the Department of the Interior. By 1940 there were 400 local housing authorities; 130,000 homes had been built.

Senator Wagner of New York revived Section 7A of the defunct Recovery Act by eliciting approval by the Congress for his National Labor Relations Act. It guaranteed the right of labor to organize and bargain collectively and forbade employers to use "unfair labor practices," defined in detail. To make sure that the law would be obeyed, it established the National Labor Relations Board. Other legislation elaborated and perpetuated protections for labor first attempted by the defunct NIRA. In 1938 the Fair Labor Standards Act established a national minimum wage and maximum hours of work; it abolished child labor under the age of sixteen.

In the meantime—in 1935—Congress had passed the Social Security Act, which authorized unemployment insurance, old-age pensions, and other benefits. These innovations not only helped the unfortunate but constituted a balance wheel for the economy, reducing somewhat the downward swings of the business cycle. In prosperous periods the amounts collected from the public to finance the benefits would exceed the outgoing payments; in recessions, the benefits paid out were greater than the governmental receipts from the insured.

The Tennessee Valley Authority: Area Planning

TVA is probably the most successful and the most celebrated of all the projects undertaken under the New Deal. The plan for it had been sketched before Roosevelt was elected in 1932, by engineers familiar with hydroelectric systems—especially Morris L. Cooke, who had retired from private practice in order to devote his time to public service. The bill authorizing TVA was introduced in Congress by Senator George Norris of Nebraska, an independent Republican progressive. Congress adopted it on May 12, 1933, early in the "first hundred days" of the Roosevelt administration.

The region drained by the Tennessee River covered parts of

five states—as much territory as a small nation—in the southern Appalachian Mountains. The average rainfall in this region was about 50 inches a year. Much of the region had been cleared of forests and underbrush and divided into small hilly farms, so that the soil was not held by roots during spring thaws and freshets. To the rivers at the bottom of the valleys, precipitation brought fertile soil, but frequent floods not only carried away houses but deposited silt in what might have been channels for river transport. The immense energy of the water flow, unharnessed by dams and turbines, went to waste. Here was a challenge to modern engineering, one that involved the building of dams to form a series of lakes, channels, and hydroelectric power stations, the introduction of efficient agriculture and forestry, and the attraction of manufacturing plants as a source of employment.

Privately owned electric utility companies waged a bitter war against the plan by lobbying, publicity, and lawsuits, but they failed to destroy it. The TVA controlled the generation of power, and sold it for distribution not only to municipalities and cooperative associations but to privately owned distributing companies. Under the law creating the agency, it had the right to set maximum retail prices charged by the distributors. The more kilowatts it was able to deliver, the lower became the maximum retail price. Yet the volume of sales increased so rapidly that even the privately owned utility distributing companies made larger profits than before. TVA itself amortized its investments in the course of time, paid to local governments the equivalent of the taxes they would have levied if the authority had been privately owned, and eventually earned a substantial return for the federal government. Over the years, TVA brought higher standards of living to the population of the region, restored the forests, and made possible better agricultural practices. Its own investments in construction during the depression played a large role in increasing employment and stimulating economic recovery. It was, and remains, the most striking single success of the New Deal. But appropriate area planning in other regions, rural or urban, still presents difficulties, and opportunities.

Reciprocal Trade Agreements

Despite his action in reducing the gold content of the dollar, President Roosevelt was opposed to high protective tariffs such as the Republicans had instituted. Secretary of State Cordell Hull also favored low import duties and advised the President to ask for new legislation to supplant the Smoot-Hawley Act. In addition, he drastically revised the method of arriving at the specific rates. Under the traditional process Congress specified the amount of duty on each commodity; this gave rise to "log-rolling." Each legislator tried to obtain higher duties for industries in his district and often obtained them by agreeing to vote for higher duties in other regions. Secretary Hull advised that the rate-making power be shifted to the executive branch of the government, to be administered by the State Department. He also suggested that tariffs be lowered by agreement with other nations to reduce their import duties in return. Congress in 1933 passed the Reciprocal Trade Agreements Act, which authorized the new method. It allowed a 50-per-cent reduction of any duty.

Before the outbreak of World War II in 1939, reciprocal agreements of this sort were signed with twenty-six nations, and United States exports thereafter increased more rapidly than imports. The reduction of barriers to foreign trade extended to many more than the twenty-six nations who signed reciprocal agreements, since the United States already had treaties with many other nations, according to which reduction of import duties granted to the "most favored nation" must also affect the signatories of the treaties.

The Record of Deficit Spending

Under the Hoover administration the federal budget was balanced, with a small surplus, in fiscal years 1929 and 1930 (fiscal years begin in June). In 1931 a deficit of $462 million appeared— small in comparison with subsequent deficits. In 1932 the deficit jumped to $2735 million; net tax receipts fell by nearly $2000 million—it was the bottom year of the depression. Then, under the first New Deal, the deficits were never less than in fiscal year

1933, at $2602 million, and became $4425 million in 1936. In 1937 the deficit suddenly diminished to $2777 million, and in 1938 dropped even further, to $1777 million.

Now let us look at employment. The number of wage and salary workers with jobs in non-agricultural establishments, which had been 31,339,000 in 1929, fell to a low of 23,628,000 in 1933. From that point it rose year by year to 31,026,000 in 1937, and fell off again to 29,209,000 in 1938. Unemployment comprised only 3 per cent of the civilian labor force in 1929, but it rose year by year to 24.9 per cent in 1933. Then the percentage of unemployed diminished year by year to 14.3 per cent in 1937. Suddenly, in 1938, it rose to 19 per cent. Thereafter, it declined again until it reached an absolute minimum in the Second World War.

What happened in 1937 and 1938? Obviously a sharp recession in 1938 followed the reduction of deficit spending in 1937 and accompanied the even greater drop in 1938. One important factor in this decline of the deficit can be accounted for by the newly established Social Security. On January 1, 1937, the payroll taxes from the insured began to flow into the trust funds administered by the federal government, but as yet no benefits were being paid. This accounts for a large part of the 1937 diminution of deficit spending.

The recession of 1937 and 1938 was derived also from a drop in private investment. In dollars having the same purchasing power as in 1954, business investment fell from $27 billion in 1937 to $15.5 billion in 1938, thus sharply diminishing the national income. The decline was largely in "producers' durable equipment" and in business inventories. Two kinds of influence go far to account for this slump of private investment. One was the temporary policy of the Federal Reserve Board in curbing business loans. The system had recently received increases in its gold reserve, and its governors, for some reason that the New Deal economists could not understand, feared inflation, and so discouraged loans to business. The other influence was the bitter hostility of big business toward the New Deal, expressed not only in litigations against governmental attempts to dissolve utility holding companies, but in nationwide publicity and lobbying, carried on by organizations such as the "Liberty League." Loans and investments by the banking system fell from $39.6 billion in 1936 to $38.4 billion in 1937. In 1938 they rose to $40.7 billion.

In 1939, the last year not affected by preparation for hostilities in World War II, gross private investment rose from the $6.7 billion of 1938 to $9.3 billion. The federal deficit increased from $2 billion to $2.2 billion.

In dollars of constant value (at 1954 prices) the totals of the Gross National Product were:

	(*In billions*)
1933	$126.6
1934	138.5
1935	152.8
1936	173.3
1937	183.5
1938	175.1
1939	189.3

If we assume that 1935 is the last year of the first New Deal, the gain of GNP in its three years was $26.2 billion, in spite of the failure of NRA. Thereafter, the second New Deal increased GNP by $36.5 billion in five years. Deficit spending existed in both periods; the only setback occurred in 1938, when deficit spending stumbled.

CHAPTER 11

War Spending
Brings Full Employment

In September 1939, when the Second World War broke out in Europe, the unemployed members of the labor force in the United States still numbered about 10 million.

For some two years before that, the danger of war had been increasing because of the rise of the dictators, Hitler in Germany and Mussolini in Italy, and their seizures of territory. The need of other possible victims might have stimulated a boom in American war industries similar to that which occurred between 1914 and 1917 when Britain, France, and other European belligerents in World War I had depended on supplies from the United States, long before this country entered the conflict. But Congress, disillusioned by the peace treaties of Versailles and the Trianon, and disturbed by the difficulty of collecting foreign war debts, decided to prevent any new pressures which might arise from American involvement in the production of munitions for export.

The Neutrality Acts forbade loans from the United States government or its citizens to belligerent nations; if they wanted to buy munitions in this country they would have to pay cash. (This virtually blocked all exports of war supplies, since there would be no way in which foreign nations could get the necessary dollars.) Ships under American registry were forbidden to carry munitions; thus there could be no incidents like the sinkings of American vessels which had preceded our entrance to World War I. American citizens were forbidden to travel in danger zones, except on official business. The practical outcome of the "cash-and-carry" legislation, so far as it was effectual (some ships canceled registration in the United States and instead registered in Panama), was to weaken the democratic forces of western Europe in their resistance to the aggression of the Axis dictators. On April 9, 1940, Hitler invaded Denmark and Norway. He attacked the Low Countries on May 10. France fell a few weeks later; British armies were defeated at Dunkirk and had to retire from Europe.

On May 16, 1940, President Roosevelt sent a message to Congress urging a massive defense program. Congress appropriated the necessary expenditure. Industry in the United States soon received huge governmental orders. The total production of goods and services, valued in dollars with constant purchasing power, increased 15 per cent between 1940 and 1941, and another 15 per cent in 1941 and 1942, before and after the Japanese attack on Pearl Harbor. By 1944 the real national product was far above that of 1940. Unemployment had virtually disappeared; it was replaced by scarcity of labor. In 1944, also, civilian consumers bought 15 per cent more than in 1940, in spite of the fact that the output of war industries in 1944 was more than thirteen times as large as in 1940 and that nearly eleven million persons were in the armed forces.

The inference to be drawn from these facts is that large deficit spending by the government can, under appropriate circumstances, diminish unemployment and increase the incomes of the citizens. It happened during a major war, but it can also occur when the nation is at peace. If the government had imposed taxes on the public large enough to cover its expenditures, that would have merely taken money out of one pocket to put it in another. But, as actually occurred, if the money which government spends is in large part created by the banking system (and thus is not taxed away from the consumers), the consumers will obviously have more money to spend than before.

The supply of money—that is, of deposits in banks and of currency outside banks—increased by $77.6 billion between 1939 and 1944 inclusive. In the same period government securities held by the banking system increased by $78.1 billion— slightly more than the increase of currency outside banks, that is, of the money circulating among individuals, business concerns, and public agencies. The increase in the money supply therefore came largely from new issues of government securities held by the banking system as collateral for bank loans or bought outright by commercial banks. The federal government also issued some non-marketable securities such as savings bonds; these issues temporarily diminished the money in possession of the lenders, who were not permitted to sell the bonds or offer them as collateral for bank loans. In that respect, their effect on the current money supply was much the same as increased taxes.

The conservatives who in the 1930s and 1940s argued that a large and growing national debt would bring ruin were not thinking as Alexander Hamilton did in 1790, when the gross federal debt was $75,463,000 and the population of the nation was about 4 million. We remember that Hamilton wrote: "It is a well known fact in countries in which the national debt is properly funded, and an object of established confidence, it answers most of the purposes of money." The growth of the federal debt between 1932 and 1944 certainly increased the amount of money, just as it did in Hamilton's day, and this in turn eventually extinguished unemployment through governmental spending. This conclusion was so obvious that thereafter no federal budget has been adopted without consideration of its effect on employment. The experience also proves that too much deficit spending will increase prices.

Though during World War II virtually all the members of the civilian labor force had jobs, the growth of their incomes did not enable them to buy a corresponding increase of consumer goods. Consumer income nearly doubled, even after taxes were paid, but production of consumer goods rose only about 15 per cent between 1940 and 1944. Prices of these goods were increased by about 25 per cent. High prices, and in many cases scarcity, curbed consumers' purchases. The people did, however, enlarge their savings from about 5 per cent of their disposable incomes in 1939 to almost 25 per cent in 1944.

Wartime Planning

Since the government was the chief ultimate buyer, it could determine the shape of the economy. In doing so, it took advantage of the experience in World War I, for the most part imitating its successes and avoiding its mistakes.

The Neutrality Acts had forbidden loans to foreign nations that wished to buy war supplies in the United States, partly because most of these loans made in World War I had not been repaid and probably never could be. Even before the United States entered the Second World War, President Roosevelt evaded this obstacle by the policy of Lend-Lease. The United States Government would provide to its allies not the money to buy needed goods, but the goods themselves; and in return the allies would lend to the United States necessary goods which this nation might use. The same principle was applied to leases of ships, land, buildings, or offices which might be required by the armed forces. After the war was over, the books would be balanced and the debt would consist only of any difference between the contributions of the parties concerned.

Many industrial executives in the United States were reluctant to build the necessary new plants or change over existing equipment to manufacture munitions when rearmament began in 1940. They feared that they might be left, after the crisis was over, with buildings or machinery which could not be used to satisfy the needs of peacetime purchasers. In order to overcome this difficulty, the government paid for about 72 per cent of the required equipment. The companies concerned had the option to buy plants and machinery so provided, after the war, paying only at such a highly accelerated depreciation that the equipment would be costless to the purchaser long before it had been worn out.

War Planning Agencies

After some fumbling with the competition of the various military services buying munitions and supplies, the government created a new version of the War Industries Board of World War I. On January 13, 1942, it set up the War Production Board, "with full and final authority over all American production." This agency adopted a production program covering all the needs, both civilian and military, of the United States and its allies; it issued priorities, allocated scarce materials, and allocated the final products.

One important difference between the War Industries Board of World War I and the War Production Board of World War II was the promptness with which the latter learned its task. It was created less than a month after the United States was plunged into war by the Japanese attack in December 1941. The experience of the War Industries Board in learning its job was not forgotten. The War Production Board immediately made a national inventory of the necessary materials and of the capacities of various industries. It understood the necessity of priorities and allocation. One advantage over its prototype was that it held final authority not only over war industries but also "over all American production." This clause in its charter meant mainly inclusion of consumers' goods as well as of munitions—with the exception of agricultural products, which remained under AAA. Farmers, under that agency, provided enough food and fibers. Other civilian goods the board limited in so far as the goods interfered with essential production. The outstanding example was the cessation of manufacture of passenger automobiles, since the industry was busy with military equipment—for example, tanks and jeeps. Here was central planning indeed.

Another advantage of the War Production Board was that it could be manned largely by trained personnel of the New Deal —economists, lawyers, administrators. Some whose direct planning experience had consisted of trying to manage Title I of the National Recovery Administration, abolished by the Supreme Court, could now work in a governmental agency which had greater powers and unquestionably constitutional authority. Governmental workers in several other New Deal agencies—notably the WPA—were given their "honorable discharge in wartime" by President Roosevelt in April 1942. We had no longer any need to try to find work for the jobless or carry on relief for the unemployed. The problem now was not to keep the labor force employed, but rather to find enough workers. The administrators of these agencies were well equipped to use their talents in planning for the needs of war.

Permanent New Deal agencies such as the Tennessee Valley Authority and the Agricultural Adjustment Administration played valuable roles in the war economy. In the TVA area there existed a large supply of electric power available at low cost to industry —and also to the development of atomic energy. AAA no longer needed to limit drastically the output of farm products, but it could emphasize the application of the farmers' resources to the crops which were most needed.

"Bits and Pieces"

Some engineers on the staff of the War Production Board, noting the immense orders for munitions which went out to the big corporations such as General Motors, became concerned about small business firms of high quality scattered about the nation which were capable of producing "bits and pieces" useful in the assembly lines but not fully utilized. The giant concerns often owned plants to supply such parts, and expanded their output instead of ordering from the smaller but competent firms. This was economic waste, especially when the demand for munitions exceeded the supply. In some instances large producers of the finished articles made subcontracts for parts with the smaller, independent shops. In these cases the waste of idle capacity might be avoided, but the small concern would not be capable of the bargaining possible in a competitive market, since often there was only one buyer. Should not the WPB supervise these contracts? And what would happen to the small firms when peace came? Concern over giant companies and monopoly not only existed in the War Production Board but was felt in other governmental agencies such as the Tennessee Valley Authority. Where a few large concerns tended to control prices, as in automobiles and steel, the New Dealers, now working in war agencies, welcomed such new independent producers as Kaiser with his jeep.

Price-Control and Rationing

Noting the rise in prices caused by an increase of personal incomes more rapid than output of consumer goods, Congress passed on January 30, 1942, a bill setting up the Office of Price Administration, with power to regulate retail prices and ration the sales of scarce commodities. Prices of agricultural products, primarily food, had not risen enough to be in "parity" with other prices, and so were exempted for the time being. They rose above parity before the end of the war.

Food costs constitute a large part of consumer budgets, and so unions demanded higher wage rates as food prices rose. Strikes and threats of strikes were a threat to maximum industrial output. The government therefore created a National War Labor Board and persuaded employers and unions to accept compulsory arbitration. And the President on October 3, 1942, ordered the Board to freeze wages, as of the previous September 15, with some exceptions to eliminate "substandards of living," and to permit a 15-per-cent increase over the wage levels of January 1941 to those who had not already received it. In April 1943 all further increases were forbidden. Since not only the full peacetime labor force but many retired workers, women, and others not previously seeking employment now had paid jobs, and since no further expansion of the labor force could be expected, average weekly working hours increased from less than 40 to 45.2 in manufacturing, and to 43.4 in coal mining. Similar increases in the work week occurred in construction.

As in World War I, the railroads were overburdened with traffic and needed to be operated as if they were a national unit. This time it was not necessary that the government operate them, as it had in World War I; that experience was so well remembered that the carriers now voluntarily submitted to the planning of the Office of Defense Transportation, which also controlled other means of transport.

The Reconstruction Finance Corporation, created in 1932 under President Hoover as a means of governmental aid for banks and business concerns in trouble because of the depression, and expected by him to be dissolved in six months, still existed in the 1940s and was used by the government in financing expansion of production for a global war. An Export-Import Bank, owned by the federal government, supplied funds for development of such trade with foreign countries as was needed to obtain enough war materials—for example, tin from Bolivia. A Board of Economic Warfare was concerned not only with obtaining strategic materials but with keeping them out of the hands of enemies. It did this by building up stocks of scarce metals and chemicals in the United States. "Stockpiling" became routine and it continued after peace came.

One curious development illustrates the distortion of war demand. The use of copper so increased that this normally abundant metal became "scarce." In order to save copper, the electric utilities began to use silver instead in their pole connections. Copper pennies were not minted for the duration of the emergency; the wartime pennies were made of steel.

"The Miracle of Production"

Government purchases of goods and services rose from $13.1 billion in 1939 to $96.5 billion in 1944, that is, more than seven times. War expenditures of the federal government account for about 45 per cent of everything that was bought. Some of the money came from higher tax yields, not only because the rates were higher but also because of the growth in personal and business income and the increase in civilian employment from 48 million in 1940 to 54 million in 1944. (Meanwhile the armed forces had absorbed 10.9 million recruits.) But a larger part of governmental spending was financed by loans on the part of the banking system, which, as has been said, increased its holdings of government securities by $78.1 billion.

The value of total output of goods and services in the United States rose, after eliminating the effect of increase in prices, from $97.1 billion in 1940 to $167.6 billion in 1944. This four-year gain was an increase of $70.5 billion, or about 73 per cent. An analysis by the Twentieth Century Fund estimates that $44.5 billion of the rise was due to more people working, $14.9 billion to longer hours of work, and $11.1 billion to other causes.

This dramatic success included temporary abolition of unemployment, production of the goods most needed by the nation and its citizens, and fair distribution of the limited products available to civilians. It did not, however, rest on a social revolution, civil war, or the application of Marxist dogmas interpreted and revised by a Lenin or a Stalin. Private ownership of the means of production not only remained but was rescued from the doldrums of economic depression. On the other hand, free and democratic organizations of labor preserved and enlarged their power to bargain with employers, within the guidelines necessary to maintain full production and check inflation of prices.

If this much could be done when a large part of the nation's output consisted of instruments of destruction, what might not be accomplished if planning could be used as fruitfully, by application of suitable means, for the nation's welfare in peace? Could we not tame speculative booms followed by depressions? Could we not so increase the nation's output of nonmilitary production as to conquer poverty and provide a better life for all?

CHAPTER 12

Planning for Peace

As the end of the war approached, the New Dealers, who had used planning first to attack the Great Depression and later to manage the war economy, began to think seriously about policies after the return of peace.

There were two main schools of thought about what might be expected when the war economy was demobilized, if the federal government did not adopt appropriate action. One school expected the return of unemployment and depression. Many wage-earners had been out of work throughout the 1930s, before war spending ended unemployment. Millions in the armed services would be discharged when peace came, and so would be thrown on the civilian labor market. Military spending would be drastically cut. High tax receipts would soon extinguish the budgetary deficit, and so deficit spending would no longer stimulate the economy. Forecasts of the number who would seek work, and of the probable number of civilian jobs, indicated that there would be many more applicants than jobs.

The other school of thought (a small minority) expected full employment, and possibly even a price inflation like that of 1919 and 1920 after World War I. They believed that the discharge of those in the armed services would not greatly swell the civilian labor force, because many women wage-earners would return to housekeeping, elderly men who had escaped the draft because of their age, but had worked in war industries, would now seek retirement under Social Security, and many of the younger veterans would wish to continue their education, if given the opportunity. The number of jobs for labor, though diminished on one hand by cessation of armament production, would be augmented on the

other by an immense increase in consumers' demand for new passenger automobiles not manufactured since 1942, for better
housing, and for other durable goods. War rationing had limited
purchasing by consumers; at the same time they had received the
wages of full employment and in many cases pay for overtime as
well. Many had increased their savings and would have ready
cash to spend for goods that were scarce before 1946. As we shall
see, the forecast of those who expected the principal economic
danger of peace to be not unemployment but inflation was correct.

Whatever the outcome might be, the nation would need an
agency qualified to recommend policies demanded by the situation. Some of the New Dealers devoted their thinking mainly to a
permanent system of economic planning able to guide the nation
according to the needs of the changing economic scene. A permanent planning institution might assess the state of the economy
continually, year by year or month by month, and recommend
both to governmental agencies and to private concerns the policies
required for the maintenance and growth of a healthy economy.

The tools available to such an agency had been hammered out
to a considerable extent by research on the part of economists
and statisticians. The accounting required to calculate the amount
of the national income, its changes up or down, and its composition, was ready for use. Wesley Mitchell, the leader in statistical
analysis of the business cycle, with his collaborators at the National
Bureau of Economic Research, had made significant advances in
our understanding of this phenomenon. Much had been learned
about monetary management by the banking system, and about
the effects of governmental fiscal policy. Reliable estimates of
employment and unemployment could be currently made because
a system of federal employment agencies existed in which wage-
earners must register in order to be insured against joblessness.

The Transition to a Peacetime Economy

When the war ended in 1945, the federal administration, supported by a large majority of the citizens, prepared for the transition to a peacetime economy. They did not intend to abandon
what had been learned from the sudden change-over to "business

as usual" when World War I ended in 1918. The lessons learned from the New Era of the 1920s, which led to the calamitous depression beginning in 1929, were fresh in the minds of citizens and elected officials. And the political administrators of the nation were largely the same as those who had been leaders in the New Deal of the 1930s, had experimented with national economic planning, and had guided the World War II "miracle of production."

The dominant opinion among the citizens and their elected representatives did not favor destruction of private business enterprise or of the role played by the competition of free markets in determining production and prices. The public had learned by recent experience, however, that government may and usually must supplement business enterprise by preventing abuses of private power, by stimulating economic growth, by minimizing unemployment, by cushioning the vibrations of the economy between booms and depression, and by seeking democratic social goals. The sort of regime which seemed necessary was neither pure capitalism nor socialism, but what has come to be called a "mixed economy."

Demobilization

Between 1944, when war costs were at their peak, and 1946, the first full year after the return of peace, war expenditures of the federal government were reduced by more than 80 per cent. The decline (at 1950 prices) amounted to about $110 billion.

The discharged members of the armed forces were not left to fend for themselves, as in 1919. The nation now had unemployment insurance, with a system of public employment agencies. Veterans were allowed to register at the employment offices and received unemployment compensation until they found jobs. Those who wished to start businesses or farms of their own could obtain bank loans, which were guaranteed by the federal government. Even better, veterans who wished to do so could complete their education, a purpose for which government grants were available. Many took advantage of this opportunity; faculties of colleges and universities discovered that these earnest and usually intelligent young men greatly improved the work of their fellow students. The veterans who needed physical or mental treatment were aided by federal veterans' hospitals.

The Office of Price Administration continued to protect consumers against increases in prices due to scarcity of consumers' goods, thus checking the tendency to inflation or to speculating for a rise in inventory values, such as had occurred in 1919 and 1920. Rationing, however, was abandoned. Savings of the citizens, accumulated during the war, now offered them an opportunity to buy houses, the total supply of which had not much increased during the hostilities, and new automobiles, not produced for civilians before peace came. Governmental agencies were ready to build public works and stimulate construction of dwellings. The consequence of this situation was not unemployment or depression such as many economists had expected. On the contrary, the situation created a powerful upward pressure on prices, which the Office of Price Administration tried to check. Black markets grew.

Late in 1945 a controversy between the United Auto Workers and General Motors triggered a price explosion. The workers now had smaller earnings than during the war, because they no longer worked overtime (with extra payment per hour). The union therefore demanded a higher hourly rate, arguing first, that the employer could well afford it without raising prices, and, second, that the reduction in wage earnings which had occurred, and which would probably spread throughout the economy if General Motors led the way, might bring recession in the national economy. Early in 1946 a similar dispute arose in the steel industry. In both cases strikes interfered with production at a time when the federal government wished to encourage full production and full employment. In both cases the employers refused to accept a compromise suggested by governmental fact-finding boards. President Truman surrendered, allowing the price increases demanded by the employers in automobiles and steel, in order to end the strikes.

Under the law, price-control would automatically lapse in June 1946. Congress was unable to pass an acceptable renewal of the statute and in the fall of 1946 abolished price-control altogether. Prices rose accordingly, but the real values of the Gross National Product did not. In terms of 1954 prices, the GNP diminished slightly between 1946 and 1947, the contraction being about $2 million out of $282 billion. This episode was far from being fatal, but it did illustrate the necessity of cooperation between private enterprise and government, if planning in the interest of all the citizens was to succeed. The cost-of-living index of prices paid by consumers had risen by less than 30 per cent during the war, but in the three years after peace came it increased to 70 per cent above the prewar level. Those who depended on pensions or annuities, or other income from fixed capital such as bonds or mortgages, suffered accordingly. The earners of wages and salaries were stimulated to demand increases of pay, in order to avoid loss in purchasing power.

The Employment Act of 1946

The experience of the nation with the wide fluctuations of prosperity and depression during the preceding thirty years had by this time convinced leaders of action, as well as leaders of thought, that permanent national economic planning must be adopted. President Franklin D. Roosevelt had been converted to the idea, and after his death President Harry Truman carried out the project. The planning must, of course, govern the economic policies of the federal government, which now occupied a powerful role in the decisions which would affect the national economy. And it must have also the understanding and cooperation of the states and of business management, labor, agriculture, education, and other professions.

Congress passed the Employment Act in 1946, the year after the war ended. Its purpose was described in the following paragraph:

> The Congress hereby declares that it is the continuing policy and responsibility of the Federal Government to use all practicable means consistent with its needs and obligations and other essential considerations of national policy, with the assistance and cooperation of industry, agriculture, labor, and state and local governments, to coordinate and utilize all its plans, functions, and resources for the purpose of creating and maintaining, in a manner calculated to foster and promote free competitive enterprise and the general welfare, conditions under which there will be afforded useful employment opportunities, including self employment, to those able, willing and

seeking to work, and to promote maximum employment, production and purchasing power.

The law required that the President submit to Congress, at the beginning of each of its sessions, an economic report on the current situation, with a suggested program for implementing the policy of the act. It also created a Council of Economic Advisers, consisting of three men subordinate to the President, with a professional staff, to report to him the condition of the nation's economy and suggest action to be taken. The council is in close touch with members of the Executive Office and other governmental departments and agencies. In its report of 1965 the council listed no less than twenty governmental committees and four international organizations in whose deliberations it had participated. The council also consults regularly with business, labor, agricultural, and consumer organizations.

A joint committee of the House and Senate reviews the annual Economic Report of the President; this committee is required by law to state its views on the President's recommendations and to sponsor bills to carry out such of them as the joint committee may approve. The committee also holds its own hearings on the conditions of the national economy.

The Employment Act became law and began its work during the administration of President Truman. It was continued during the terms in office of Presidents Eisenhower, Kennedy, and Johnson. Each chose his own Economic Council; Democrats and Republicans accepted the responsibility of economic planning as defined in the Employment Act. Congress, with its Joint Economic Committee, performed its duties as required by the statute. The annual Economic Report of the President (and occasionally an interim report) has been read by editors, legislators, economists, business executives, labor officials, representatives of agriculture, and other leaders of opinion. Even if the Employment Act had not affected national policy directly, it would still have provided carefully prepared summaries of the existing situation and basic guidelines of economic activity. The citizens are not likely again to assume, as many did in the 1920s, that private enterprise, left to its own devices, will maintain lasting prosperity.

CHAPTER 13

The Longest Period of Prosperity

In the twenty years that followed the end of World War II, there were four recessions, each of short duration. Measured in 1964 prices, the Gross National Product fell from $337.9 billion in 1946, the first full year of peace, to $336.8 billion in 1947. In 1948 it rebounded to $350.4 billion. (The Economic Council did not exist before 1946.) The second recession brought a decline from $448.9 billion in 1953 to $439.8 billion in 1954. Recovery brought it back to $473.4 billion in 1955. The third began with a decline of the Gross National Product from $493.0 billion in 1957 to $486.0 billion in 1958. In 1959 recovery had raised the GNP to $518.1 billion. A slight recession in 1960 and 1961 appears in the annual totals only as a retardation of the growth of the national product.

The record of personal disposable income—in 1964 prices—reflected the mild nature of these recessions. "Disposable" income is what is left after paying taxes. Per-capita disposable income—a figure obtained by dividing the total of disposable personal income by the number of persons in the nation—declined slightly between 1946 and 1949 and did not recover to the level achieved during the war until 1950. But after that it rose substantially, being interrupted only by a drop from $1833 in 1953 to $1815 in 1954, and from $1968 in 1957 to $1957 in 1958. By 1964 it had risen to $2248. Thus, if a family of three in 1964 received the "average" personal disposable income, it would have had spending money, after paying taxes, of $6744.

There still were, however, many "poor" families. The 1965 Economic Report defined them as families which have total money incomes of less than $3000 (in 1962 dollars). Nine million, or 19 per cent of the nation's families, were in this category in 1963. Nevertheless, the number of poor families had declined from 34 per cent of all families in 1949 to 19 per cent in 1963, or from 13.4 million to 9 million. Unfortunate individuals without families are even poorer. There were 5 million of these in 1963 with incomes of less than $1500.

It would be difficult to discover any previous period of seventeen years in the history of the United States in which recessions were so brief and mild and economic recovery was so strong.

The long-term upward thrust of the nation's output depends largely on gains in productivity, defined in the Economic Report as average output per man-hour of work. The index of productivity, so defined for the total private sector of the economy, is based on 100 for the years 1957 to 1959. This index shows a gain of output per man-hour from 70.9 in 1947 to 120.5 in 1964. The advance, of course, depends only in part on the skills of the wage-earners. Management, and investment in more efficient equipment, made it possible. In a chapter on "Perspectives," the 1965 Report of the Council of Economic Advisers declared:

> If the average rate of productivity gains until the year 2000 no more than match those of the last seventeen years, output per man-hour will be three times as great as that today. If working hours and labor force participation rates were to remain unchanged, average family income would approximate $18,000 (in today's prices). Undoubtedly, some part of these potential gains in income will be taken in the form of greater leisure—through some combination of shorter hours, later entry into the labor force, and earlier retirement. If the advance in productivity should speed up—as many project—gains in income or leisure could be even greater.

Stimulating Economic Growth

Chapter 1 of the 1965 report of the Council of Economic Advisers analyzed "the sustained expansion of 1961-1964," which, at the time when the report was written, had already continued for a longer period than the two preceding expansions and had reached a higher level.

There had been a slowing of the upward movement in 1962;

on the advice of the Council, President Kennedy in August of that year announced that he would ask Congress in 1963 to reduce tax rates on personal income and corporate profits. Such a bill was enacted in February 1964. In the meantime the government supported an expansive monetary policy, so that business would be able to finance enlarged investment in the means of production at a low cost: bank credit was "easy." Between the fourth quarter of 1963 and the fourth quarter of 1964, business invested in plant and equipment (fixed investment) enough to increase it by 9 per cent.

The new tax bill also reduced taxes on individual incomes. Consumers purchase roughly two-thirds of the nation's output; the tax cut enlarged their purchases, since about 93 per cent of consumers' disposable income is spent for goods and services. There was neither speculation in inventories caused by any expectation of higher prices, nor inadequacy of inventories to fulfill final sales of goods. Wholesale prices remained unusually stable. Corporate profits increased steadily. Total compensation of employees, rising by 26 per cent between the first quarter of 1961 and the third quarter of 1964, remained close to 71 per cent of the total national income. Productivity rose steadily, and to a greater degree than in the two previous expansions; as a consequence, unit labor costs remained unchanged for the private economy as a whole and were slightly reduced in manufacturing. This indicates that in collective wage-bargaining both unions and employers, on the average, followed the guideposts of the federal government, which urge increase of hourly wage rates by the same percentage as the nationwide gain in output per man-hour.

Although consumer prices increased about 1.2 per cent a year between 1960 and 1964, the price index does not take account of improvements in the quality of goods or of increase in the services of governmental agencies. Correction for such omissions might offset, at least in part, the slow upward drift of the index of consumer prices.

A large part of the recent resistance to recessions may be attributed to what are called built-in (or automatic) stabilizers. Government purchases do not decrease during a recession as do purchases of business or individuals. Meanwhile tax collections fall as profits and wages decline. There is an increase in "transfer payments"—that is, payments of unemployment insurance and Social Security—and a decrease in the contributions of individuals and employers to the funds out of which these benefits are paid.

The government can reinforce the effect of the automatic stabilizers on the purchasing power of consumers by reducing tax rates and increasing its expenditures. The council recommended for this purpose in 1965 a reduction of excise taxes on numerous articles, with a total saving to consumers of about $1.75 billion, and an increase of Social Security benefits amounting to $3.5 billion. Both recommendations were embodied in bills that, with some amendments, were passed by Congress.

In the fiscal year ending June 30, 1964, the federal government received in cash $115.5 billion and paid in cash to the public $120.3 billion—a stimulus to the economy of $4.8 billion. It was then estimated that in fiscal year 1965 the incoming payments would be $117.4 billion and the outgoing payments $121.4 billion—a net stimulus of $4 billion—while in fiscal 1966 the incoming payments would be $123.5 billion and the outgoing $127.4 billion, a stimulus of $3.9 billion. These cash figures include not only tax receipts on one hand and governmental appropriations on the other, but also the collection and expenditure of Social Security trust funds. The estimated decline of the yearly cash deficit would indicate that as employment rises the government receives more in taxes and in contributions to the trust funds, while it pays out less in unemployment insurance and relief.

Such estimates, however, are seldom wholly exact. It turned out that in fiscal 1965 the net deficit of the government was only $2.7 billion instead of the estimated $4 billion. In fiscal 1966, however, the net excess of payments by the federal government was much larger than expected and provided a stimulus to the economy of $6.9 billion. For fiscal 1967 the inauguration of Medicare for elder citizens would greatly increase the expenditure for Social Security. With all those billions contributed by government to the economy, consumers would have more money to spend, but they would not necessarily receive more consumption goods for their money. Rising prices might very well wipe out their gains. The index of prices for March 1966, as compared with that for March 1965, already showed an increase in food prices of 6.2 per cent, with somewhat smaller increases in other retail prices; the rise of all prices averaged 2.9 per cent.

Can Price Inflation Be Avoided?

When government stimulates the economy by expansive fiscal and monetary measures—that is, by distributing to the citizens more money than it collects from them and by maintaining credit policies, through the Federal Reserve System, that make it easy to borrow from the banks—the stimulus may be felt either in the production and sale of a larger amount of goods and services, or in higher prices of goods and services purchased, or in some mixture of the two. It is the aim of the planners, as a rule, to expand production and to avoid increase in prices. That policy presumably increases the demand for labor and so helps to achieve or sustain "full employment." When output is enlarged, but prices do not rise, consumers benefit by obtaining more with their larger incomes. When, on the other hand, the effect of governmental stimulus is to raise prices more than it increases production, the only gainers are the processors and distributors, who can charge more for their products without incurring an equal rise in their unit costs.

According to economic theory, competition will tend to lower prices of the goods or services offered for sale when the unit costs of production are diminished. Accordingly the Employment Act specifically charges the government to "foster and promote free competitive enterprise."

In industries where efficient operation requires a large degree of monopoly, such as transportation and public utilities supplying electricity, gas, or communication by telephone or telegraph, governmental regulating agencies have long exercised jurisdiction over prices. Manufacturing companies, on the other hand, are expected to compete; agreements on prices are forbidden by the antitrust laws. In the industries that embrace many firms, competitition usually does prevail, but when there are only a few producers, agreement on prices or the tacit following of a price leader may more easily occur.

There has been a marked decline in competition since World War II, chiefly as a result of business mergers. The hundred largest manufacturing firms in the nation increased their share in their respective markets from 23 per cent in 1947 to 32 per cent in 1962. In a number of fields—aluminum, locomotives, tin cans and tinware, cigarettes, computers, motor vehicles, tires and inner tubes, aircraft engines, and the products of steel works and rolling mills—the four largest manufacturers in each field supplied half or more of the total value of shipments. This approach to monopoly was viewed with concern by the government, which in many cases prevented mergers by prosecutions under the antitrust laws. In this connection we read in the 1965 *Economic Report*:

> Enforcement activity has been rigorous during each of the postwar Administrations, attesting to the bipartisan nature of the Nation's belief in maintaining maximum competition consistent with a productive and efficient economy. . . . More precise criteria have been developed with regard both to the structure of industry—the degree of concentration that generates excessive market power—and to the performance of industry—the abuse of market power.

Competition, no matter how much encouraged by government, will not hold prices down when money is plentiful and goods are in short supply. Then the competition is among buyers, not sellers, and it drives prices still higher. Beginning in 1965, economists warned that the current fiscal and credit policies might lead to price inflation. The danger was described by Arthur F. Burns, President of the National Bureau of Economic Research, and former chairman of the Council of Economic Advisers, in a speech in October 1965, delivered at the Carnegie Institute of Technology. In part he said:

> Prices of raw materials began advancing toward the end of 1963; but the over-all index of wholesale prices still stood at 100, on a 1957-59 base, as late as June 1964. Since then, price increases in wholesale markets have spread out over the economy, and the index

has risen 3 per cent. In recent months, the advance in wages has also shown a tendency to accelerate. Despite improvements in productivity, the labor cost per unit of output has begun to creep up in manufacturing, and it has done more than that for some time outside of manufacturing. These developments, together with the booming rates of investment in numerous industries, indications of overbuilding in the housing market, and various symptoms of deterioration in the quality of credit, are a warning that the business cycle is not yet dead.

The immediate task of managing prosperity has therefore become more exacting. It is one thing for an economy to advance steadily when it is operating at some distance from full employment. It is quite another to continue expanding when it is already operating at or close to full employment. Now that we are approaching the latter stage, the liberal monetary and fiscal policy that our government is still pursuing is likely to intensify upward pressures on both wages and prices. True, interest rates on long-term as well as short-term loans have risen modestly since mid-year, but the surging demand for credit has more than swamped the influence of higher interest rates and the expansion of bank credit has actually been accelerating. Meanwhile, the curve of federal spending, which had flattened out for a year and a half, is again moving sharply upward—in part, but by no means entirely, because of rising military costs in Vietnam. If these financial conditions continue, the extraordinary expansion of our economy since 1961—which has done so much to lift the hopes of millions of our people—may come to an inglorious end. With an inflationary psychology again spreading, the danger of overstocking or overbuilding can no longer be remote. Nor is our balance of payments in a good position to withstand another round of inflation. While a change of economic policy always involves some risk, I believe that the managers of our national prosperity will have the best chance of extending the current expansion if they will, on the one hand, deal more realistically with the structural causes of unemployment and, on the other, take steps to slow down the rate of growth of bank credit and curb for a while the increase in federal spending on civilian programs.

Dr. Burns's speech aroused great interest among economists, but, except for a rise in the Federal Reserve's rediscount rate and its requirement of higher bank reserves, there was little indication during the next year that the government had changed its taxing, spending, or credit policies.

Residual Unemployment

"Full employment," the principal goal of the Employment Act of 1946, does not mean that all members of the labor force must have jobs at any one time. Some may be shifting their residences; some may be temporarily ill; some may be in industries which are busier in one season than in others. As a rule of thumb, if only 4 per cent of the labor force is unemployed, the planners regard their duty as fulfilled. A better test would be a comparison of the number out of work with the unfilled positions offered by employers. But in any case, economists do not expect that at any one time all the seekers for jobs will have them.

In the years between 1958 and 1964 the unemployment rate never fell to the 4-per-cent level. It continuously exceeded 5 per cent, and in some years approximated 7 per cent. In prosperous 1964, gains in reducing unemployment were made, but by the end of that fiscal year 5 per cent were unemployed—3.7 million persons. Obviously, stimulating the growth of production and of the national income had not yet produced "full employment," even if it must be expected that 4 per cent of the civilian labor force will at any one time be jobless.

The Economic Advisers to the President find three reasons for unemployment above the 4-per-cent level in otherwise prosperous times. One is the rapidly increasing number of teen-agers seeking jobs, because of the "baby boom" which began after World War II. Another is discrimination against Negroes. The third consists of areas which lag behind the nation's growth in output and wealth—"areas of chronic depression." In 1960 there were 19 such areas. "In 1965, the number of 18-year-olds will increase by almost 1 million; and growth of the teen-age labor force will be approximately 500,000—double its growth in 1964. The unemployment rate for Negroes remains more than double that for whites. Unemployment is far too high in many local labor markets."

Though the *Economic Report* does not in this passage discuss the reasons for the usual preference of employers for hiring adult whites (twenty years of age or older), other studies throw light on the subject. The demand for unskilled labor has been rapidly declining because of mechanization and automation. Many white teen-agers and many Negroes have not had the education necessary to do well in the jobs which may be open. This is especially true of high-school drop-outs of both races. Discrimination against Negroes takes its heaviest toll in limiting the quality and the opportunity of education.

Between 1900 and 1964 "white-collar" workers in the United States increased from 17.6 per cent of the "economically active civilian population" to 44 per cent. Among the "blue-collar" workers, the skilled rose from 10.5 per cent to 14 per cent, the semiskilled (operatives and kindred workers) from 12.8 per cent to 19.9 per cent, while unskilled laborers decreased from 12.5 per cent to 5 per cent. Private household workers declined from 5.4 per cent to 3 per cent, while other service workers increased from 3.6 per cent to 10 per cent. Finally, the rapid gains in productivity which took place in agriculture decreased the number of farm workers from 37.5 per cent of the nation's gainfully occupied persons to 6.3 per cent. This category includes farmers, farm managers, farm foremen, and farm laborers.

In one generation, from 1940 to 1964, the part of the nation's work force which had 8 years or less of education dropped from 50 per cent to 23 per cent. In the same period those who had 13 years or more of education—in other words, graduates from high school who also went to college—increased from about 11 per cent of the civilian labor force to 22 per cent. In spite of this shift to more years of schooling, the job opportunities remain larger for the better-educated than for those who look for employment in their teens.

Bringing Up the Stragglers

Central economic planning can contribute much to broad national objectives such as economic growth, moderation of the swings of the business cycle, maintenance of approximately full employment—with the cooperation of private enterprise, a free labor movement, and intelligent citizens. In recent years, however, the planners have turned attention also to regional planning and the removal of specific handicaps within the national community.

In 1961 the Area Redevelopment Act provided grants and loans, technical assistance, and training programs to about 1100 areas where there are persistent unemployment and low incomes. Unemployment in these areas decreased from 10.4 per cent in 1961 to 8.7 per cent in 1963; some areas did so well that they ceased to need aid in 1964. The experience led to the conclusion that even better results could be obtained if larger depressed areas, with a greater variety of potential resources, could be aided. The federal administration established an Appalachian Regional Commission covering 355 counties in 11 states—a region poor for many years and recently suffering from decline of its major industry, coal mining.

Poverty is not confined, however, to areas needing redevelopment as a whole. It may be found in growing urban regions and farming communities. The Economic Opportunity Act of 1964 attacked this problem mainly by offering education, training, and work experience to young people, under Community Action Programs mobilizing local leaders, and the Job Corps operating in conservation camps and residential training centers. A work-study program offers financial assistance to college students with low incomes, by part-time employment. And thousands of unemployed fathers or other needy adults are offered work experience and training.

Equality of opportunity, often denied to Negroes, Puerto Ricans, Spanish Americans, and Indians, is rightly supported on moral grounds, but inequality also represents economic waste. The incidence of poverty among nonwhites is 40 per cent, as contrasted with 16 per cent for the white population. "It is estimated that society loses up to $20 billion per year of potential production as a result of employment discrimination and poorer educational opportunities for nonwhites," according to the 1965 *Economic Report.* "Passage of the Civil Rights Act of 1964 marked the beginning of a new era of concern for equality of opportunity."

Equally important in diminishing unemployment was the passage of an act in 1965 offering Federal subsidies for public schools, previously financed solely by states and local governments. Special services may also be aided for private schools.

Improvement of health, desirable in itself, also can strengthen the national economy. "Between 1900 and 1963," declares the *Economic Report*, "the death rate dropped from 17.2 to 9.8 per 1000 population; as a consequence, life expectancy rose from 47 years to 70 years." But the health record of the United States is not so good as that of several other countries. The failure to make full use of recent medical research is "particularly unfortunate for children, the poor, and the elderly. . . . The 15 million children of low-income families receive far less medical care than they require. . . . In 1962 only half of the elderly had any health insurance coverage, much of it inadequate. . . . The average couple spent almost 10 per cent of its already low income on medical care." Numerous recent acts of Congress have appropriated large grants for medical research, medical education, hospital construction, public health centers. And Medicare went into action on July 1, 1966.

Metropolitan Planning

In 1960, the latest year of the decennial census when this book was written, one-third of the United States population lived in 24 metropolitan areas, each containing a million or more people. Another 30 per cent of the people lived in the remaining 188 metropolitan areas. Blight and decay occur in the older, central cities of the large metropolitan regions. Suburbs confront transportation problems for commuters. Local planning agencies have to make decisions about land use, waste disposal, pollution of water and of air, housing, open spaces, and outdoor recreation. City planning is far from new, but metropolitan blight seems to spread more rapidly than adequate remedies. "The Federal Government has a responsibility to promote planning to assure that public needs are met efficiently and that federally aided local public programs will, indeed, produce a more livable and efficient urban environment," writes the Economic Council.

CHAPTER 14

New Horizons

In the societies of civilized man, continued change must be expected. Sometimes the folkways alter slowly; sometimes the changes are so rapid as to be bewildering. Neither the Soviet state, with its central planning of a socialist economy, nor the Western democracies, with their mixed economies and policy planning, can escape the need for continual analysis of the problems which confront them and the demand for discovery of appropriate measures.

Let us begin with a look at the record of Russian planning, since that is the first and most celebrated example of authoritative central planning in an economy which sought to abolish any trace of laissez faire or private enterprise.

How Well Were Soviet Plans Fulfilled?

A careful study made for the National Bureau of Economic Research (New York) by G. Warren Nutter, *The Growth of Industrial Production in the Soviet Union* (1962), estimates the percentage of planned output achieved by important industries at the end of successive five-year plans. The measurement is in terms of "value added"—that is, the difference between costs of materials and power purchased by the industry and the value of its output. Therefore it indicates the contribution made by the industry.

At the end of the first plan (1928-1932), the fulfillment for all covered products was 74 per cent of the plan. For the plan ending in 1937 the fulfillment was 76 per cent. The years between 1937 and 1945 are omitted because in this period the Soviet Union was engaged in World War II. But the plan which ended in 1950 achieved 94 per cent of the planned goals, and that which ended in 1955 did even better, with 99 per cent. Apparently both the planners and the industries were learning to improve their performance.

The various industrial groups, however, showed less accuracy than did the total economy in producing what their several plans required. Some exceeded the schedule; others fell below it. In 1932 the machinery and equipment industries turned out 102 per cent of their plan, largely because of an overfulfillment of transportation equipment amounting to 118 per cent. At the low point stood consumer goods, with only 60 per cent of the output required by the plan—57 per cent for food and allied products, and 61 per cent for textiles and allied products. Similar differences appeared in 1937; miscellaneous machinery had the best record, 99 per cent, and consumer goods the worst, with 62 per cent. Thus the aim to expand heavy industry at the expense of consumers won in this period with a vengeance; expansion was even greater than the national plan required.

In the subsequent two plans here listed, those ending in 1950 and 1955, a similar, though smaller, bias appears. In 1950 metals, fuel, and electricity all exceeded their planned output; agricultural machinery nearly equaled the goal, with 98 per cent; consumer goods fell below the mark. Textiles still were at the bottom with 88 per cent. In the plan ending in 1955, nearly all items were closer to the plan, though many were slightly above it. The greatest variations indicate dramatically the difficulties which the regime has been having with agriculture: production of agricultural machinery soared above the planned goal with an output of 126 per cent; meanwhile the Soviet peoples had to get along with only 76 per cent of the planned output of food and allied products.

Obviously the Soviet planners and producers made a rapid recovery in output after the war ended in 1945, especially in view of the loss of population and the physical havoc done by the Nazi invaders. Was this due to their planned system? Dr. Nutter presents the percentage increase in production year by year from

1950 to 1958. In no year of this period did the output of all civilian products fall below the increase of 3 per cent more than the
preceding year that was attained in 1952; in 1950 the increase
was actually 17 per cent. Between 1950 and 1958 the average
yearly gain was 7.1 per cent. Consumer goods did not lag far below the average for all countries. But other countries which experienced physical destruction and loss of life also made rapid
recovery. The growth of industrial production in France from
1945-1946 through 1950 was faster than that in the Soviet Union,
and both Japan and West Germany surpassed even that record
from 1948 to 1958. By 1958 the increase of industrial production
since 1953 was, in France, 46 per cent, in Japan, 68 per cent, in
West Germany, 51 per cent. This outcome, however, may not be
logically used by opponents of economic planning, since there was
some degree of planning in all these countries. Moreover, it was
in 1948 that the United States offered its aid to allies and former
enemies under the Marshall Plan—an offer which the Soviet
Union rejected.

Questions of Quality and of Productivity

So far our description of Soviet planning has dealt exclusively
with the quantity of production. Yet enlargement of quantity may
take place without any improvement in quality, or indeed at the
expense of quality. An executive of a manufacturing establishment fearful of losing his job if he does not produce his quota on
schedule may cut corners to save time. The calculations of Gosplan are published in quantities of items, not tests of quality. Consumers in Russia have for many years complained about the quality of goods they have to buy.

Where engineering standards are applied, and the engineers
know their business, quality can be checked. Military weapons
and spacecraft appear to be as advanced in the Soviet Union as
in the United States. But it is difficult to apply quality standards
at a cooperative or state retail store, in an economy where there
are no privately owned merchandising establishments, where
there is virtually no competition, and where prices do not respond
readily to conditions of demand and supply.

The raw figures of output cited above need correction if they are to be regarded as measurements of changes in the welfare of Soviet citizens. They do not make any allowance for changes in the size of the territory of the Soviet Union, although much territory has been annexed. Nor do they account for changes in the population. Dr. Nutter offers the following calculations of changes in output *per person* of the Soviet peoples. In the period before planning began (1913-1928) the figure is negative. There was an average loss of 0.5 per cent a year in the amount of industrial products per person. After the inauguration of planning in 1928 there has been an annual gain, though apparently a diminishing one. From 1928 to 1940 the yearly growth of civilian products per person in the population averaged 6.1 per cent. The average annual growth per person between 1940 and 1955 was 5.1 per cent. These figures are not necessarily illuminating as an indication of welfare of the people. There is doubt about the accuracy of the censuses. And, as Dr. Nutter points out, "the great loss of population through starvation in the 1920s and 1930s probably had the paradoxical result of increasing the concurrent per-capita output," because there were fewer to feed and clothe.

Another view of productivity refers to the output per unit of labor rather than per person in the population. The unit of labor may be a man-hour or a man-year. The National Bureau of Economic Research (United States) study estimates the growth of Soviet output per man-year since 1928. There was no increase by 1933, but in 1937 a gain of 22 per cent appeared, and gains continue until the latest figure available—that of 1955—with a gain of 68 per cent above 1928 in output per man-year. Official Soviet figures indicate a far more rapid increase; the difference apparently is caused by the fact that Dr. Nutter based his figures on all workers, whereas the official figures cover only production workers in large-scale industry.

Trouble in Farming

To an American it seems strange that a nation which began its economic planning when about four-fifths of its population were engaged in agriculture should have had difficulty in producing enough food staples and fibers of satisfactory quality. In the United States one has to go back to 1840 to find such a proportion of agricultural workers. In 1930, when the Soviet Union began to plan, workers on farms in the United States constituted 10,321,000 out of a total of 48,686,000 gainfully occupied persons—little more than one-fifth. By 1950 the number of farm workers in the United States had declined to 6,953,000 out of a total 58,999,000 gainfully occupied—less than one-eighth. American farmers produce so much that since the 1930s the government has had to buy such staples as grain and cotton and hold them off the market, in order to maintain parity between the prices of crops and the prices of what farmers have to buy. And the value of agricultural exports from the United States has in some recent years exceeded $4 billion.

One obstacle encountered in Soviet agriculture was, at the beginning, that nearly all the peasants were illiterate, to say nothing of their not having the educational basis that would have enabled them to understand and apply in their work modern science and technology. At least one generation would have to pass for education to accomplish its task.

Another obstacle was the difficulty of socializing the farmers. For generations the Russian peasants had wanted land of their own; some of the luckier ones had achieved it. Land-owning, to the farmer in any part of the world, seems a natural right, a necessary basis for his vocation, a status symbol. But the Communist dogma holds that land, like capital, must be owned not by individuals but by the state, in the interest of all citizens. The Soviet authorities nationalized not only the estates of the landed class but the farm land of the peasants who had managed to gain their independence.

The new organization of agriculture made use mainly of two kinds of productive units. One is the large state farm, usually involving a transfer of ownership from the former landlord to the state. The peasants who did the work experienced merely a change in employer. The executives of the state farms might (or might not) be better managers than the former landlords, but they experienced little difficulty in dealing with the workers in most cases. The other type of administrative unit is the collective farm, which combined relatively small holdings of peasants in a single productive organization run by a "chairman" and a committee of the agricultural workers. This type of unit has suffered many difficulties. At the beginning it was opposed by some of the successful peasants who held more land than their neighbors. Under the Stalin regime a large number of these presumably more competent peasants were "liquidated" or shipped off to Siberia.

The members of the collective farm are expected to work together, under the chairman, on the land now belonging to the farm as a whole. Each has a small house of his own and a small tract which he may personally use—for example, a cow pasture or a vegetable garden. Each is remunerated for his collective work by a share in the proceeds of the whole farm. Since in the early years few if any of the agricultural workers were acquainted with machinery, tractors (with drivers) were supplied by separate tractor stations to do plowing, cultivating, and harvesting at the appropriate times.

Anyone familiar with farming, not to speak of those familiar with ordinary human nature, can imagine what administrative difficulties such a plan might encounter. Apparently it has encountered most of them. The members are more interested in their individual fields than in those of the collective. How is participation in the collective work to be measured? What happens if a tractor breaks down, or does not come at the right time? Are the chairman and the committee who do the planning for the farm competent enough to make the best use of their resources? Is there any way in which the retail customers of collective farms can effectuate their needs and choices in agricultural products, as there would be in a system of private enterprise and free markets?

New Straws in the East Wind

In recent years Soviet citizens seem to have become restless concerning the quality—and also the quantity—of the goods offered to them for private use. Doubts are expressed about the need to favor heavy industries at the expense of daily necessities or luxuries; leading political figures have publicly argued that more emphasis should be placed on satisfying the consumer. At least one Soviet economist has advanced the argument that increased profit may be used as a signal that the industry receiving it should increase its output and reduce its prices, a principle direct from the theory of private-enterprise economy. Perhaps each type of regime, socialist and private enterprise, may learn something from the other.

A dispatch to *The New York Times* from Peter Grose in Moscow, August 7, 1965, reported changes in the planning of factories producing consumers' goods. About three hundred clothing factories, which account for almost one-fifth of all output of Soviet light industry, now decide their own output by "agreement with retail stores, working only on the basis of orders received, which are dictated by the demand of consumers." They receive no plans from the central planning authorities. These authorities merely check the performance of the local firms on two questions: "Did the enterprise supply the stores with goods amounting to the contracted sum? And did the factories receive their planned profits?" There is no interference with wages, number of workers and specialists needed, or cost price of the articles made. This method works well; the consumers buy the goods, and profits increase. The initiative and incentive of all concerned are augmented.

On July 9, 1965, the *New Statesman* (England) published a report by Gloria Stewart concerning the conclusions of Agenbeguan, a brilliant young economist member of the Soviet Academy of Sciences. He presented his views to the Central Committee and later embodied them in a lecture. Among his charges against central planning were the following (much condensed):

In 1963, just before the Soviet Union had to buy a large quantity of wheat from the United States, the central statistical agency published a figure for the harvested grain, 8000 million poods, which was far above the actual amount; if the figure had been correct, Russia would have been selling grain, not buying it.

Agenbeguan said that Soviet industry was more backward than that of any other developed country. As an example, he cited the machine-tool industry; although the Soviet Union has as many machine tools as the United States, half of them are always being repaired. More workers are busy maintaining the machines than are using them. Then he attacked the efficiency of the timber industry and criticized the practice of stockpiling unsalable consumer goods.

He touched an especially sensitive subject: a marked rise in unemployment, especially in small towns and the countryside. The defense industry, he believed, was one of the main reasons; it employs a quarter of the working population, while less attention is paid to the production of consumer goods of high quality. Inefficient central planning, which often ignores local capacities and conditions, was a main target of his attack. Management, he concluded, must be given its head.

Miss Stewart wrote that Kosygin, who was second in the power structure of the Soviet Union and was the head of the government, thought highly of Agenbeguan's report.

Gains in industrial production from 1953 to 1961, measured solely in quantity, were larger in the Soviet Union than in the United States. There are several good reasons for this, mainly the fact that large areas of Soviet territory had been invaded and bombed by Hitler's armies, whereas the United States was not invaded and had little war damage to repair. During the same period the percentage gain in output of industry also exceeded that of the United States in non-Communist countries such as Japan, West Germany, Italy, and Austria. France made an economic recovery less in percentage terms than that of the Soviet Union in this period, but more than that of the United States. So did other nations such as Norway, the Netherlands, Sweden, Belgium, Canada, and the United Kingdom. Each of these nations developed its own method of economic planning. None ignored markets, profits of private enterprise, or professional management.

The Communist Satellites

Nations on the borders of Russia, for a time independent, but attached to the Soviet Union under the rule of Stalin, have adopted varieties of Communism which contain innovations not always pleasing to the Moscow government. Poland, Czechoslovakia,

Yugoslavia, Rumania, and Hungary: each has some degree of independence and is not subordinate to the planning authorities of the Soviet Union. All carry on important foreign trade; all are influenced, in one way or another, by the markets for their goods. In Yugoslavia, for example, the earnings of the industrial unit are shared with its workers, who elect their manager on the basis of his skill in providing a profit. Production plans are presented to a central bank, which finances them if they are approved. The judgments of the bank rest largely on "input-output" analysis, a technique originally worked out by a member of the faculty of Harvard University, Professor Leontieff.

United States Planning in Retrospect

We have seen in the course of this book that the United States Government has at all times followed plans of some sort that were directed toward the economic welfare of its citizens. The record goes back to Washington's first administration. Both Hamilton and Jefferson were members of his cabinet, and both had their economic plans for the nation. Hamilton's were more detailed and favored the mercantile interests, while Jefferson's land policy (culminating long after his death in the Homestead Act of 1862) was designed to benefit the now vanishing class of yeoman farmers. During the forty years that followed the Civil War, planning was held to a minimum, largely because of the notion that competition, if unchecked and unlimited, would lead to the benefit of all. Except for high protective tariffs, adopted in violation of this principle, and except for gifts of land to the new transcontinental railroads, the principal federal measure in the economic field was the Sherman Act of 1890, passed in an effort to restrain the trusts and thereby maintain free competition.

Theodore Roosevelt engaged in well-publicized efforts to dissolve the "bad" trusts, though prosecutions were hampered by court decisions narrowly restricting the Sherman Act. A more fruitful activity of his two administrations, which we have not discussed, was the first serious attempt to conserve natural resources by extending the system of national forests. The first Wilson administration presided over a number of economic reforms, including the

Sixteenth Amendment (income tax), the Federal Trade Commission, and the Federal Reserve Banks. We have seen that the first comprehensive and, for all its shortcomings, generally effective system of planning was established in Wilson's second term, during World War I. But the system was dismantled as soon as the war ended, and what ensued was the New Era of high profits and unchecked speculation that ended with the Great Depression.

Hoover had plans for restoring prosperity, but, while extending federal aid to banks and railroads, his plans failed to put purchasing power into the hands of those who needed it most, and hence they could not halt the downward spiral of deflation. The second Roosevelt did halt the spiral, and in his first two administrations the Gross National Product rose by about 50 per cent, but as late as 1939 there were still 10 million unemployed. During his first hundred days in office Congress passed a great number of measures, some of which proved to be lasting economic reforms. But the efforts of the New Deal to introduce comprehensive planning into agriculture (by the Agricultural Adjustment Act) and into industry (by the National Industrial Recovery Act) were both declared unconstitutional by the Supreme Court, and even before the Court's decision NIRA had come to be regarded as unworkable. The degree of recovery achieved by the New Deal was owed chiefly to federal relief, federal construction, and in general to federal spending, which pumped billions of dollars into the economy.

Full prosperity returned with World War II, which, on the economic side, was a second example of comprehensive and effective planning. This time the legislators had learned the lesson of 1919 and they did not deprive the government of its economic powers as soon as hostilities ended. Instead they provided for an orderly transition from war to peace, and for the first time they created machinery for peacetime planning in the shape of a Council of Economic Advisers. The sort of economic planning that the advisers have recommended does not involve government ownership of industry and control of incomes, as in the Communist countries, or the fixing of prices and standards by trade associations, as was attempted in 1933 under the National Recovery Administration. Instead it contemplates an over-all direction of the economy by adjusting rates of taxation, amounts of government spending, and the availability and cost of credit. Such measures, based on economic forecasts it is now possible to make with the improved statistical tools developed during the depression, have proved successful for twenty years in maintaining a high level of growth and prosperity.

That is the long story of planning in the U.S.A. as this book has tried to present it. But a planning agency will never lack for new problems, and some of these, both in this country and abroad, have been growing more and more urgent.

Some Problems for the Planners

The United States in recent years has had a deficit in its international payments, which has led to a substantial decrease in the nation's stock of gold. If the deficit continues year by year, it might lead to speculative raids against the value of the dollar. Great Britain has been worried about the value of the pound. The International Monetary Fund, established after World War II to prevent the devaluation of national currencies by making loans to the needy nations, may not have sufficient resources to make the loans, owing to the limited supply of gold and owing to the weakness of the dollar and the pound, which are usually accepted in place of gold.

Another urgent problem is the economic weakness of the so-called "underdeveloped countries" in Africa, Asia, and parts of Latin America. It was believed after World War II that those nations could be helped to start new industries, increase their production of food, and so raise their standards of living. Much help has been forthcoming, especially from the United States, though also from France, Britain, and Russia, among others. But the population of the "underdeveloped countries" has grown as fast as their Gross National Products—in some cases faster—with the result that the gap in living standards has widened between them and the industrialized nations, including Japan. Poor and hungry nations are faced with continual threats to internal stability and themselves become a threat to international peace.

Vastly more ominous for the future is the population explosion. Even what may seem like a small percentage growth per year in the number of human beings would eventually produce so many that there would not be food enough, or even water enough, to sustain them. In that case we might expect a fate against which Malthus warned some two centuries ago—a limitation of population by famine, pestilence, and war. Incidentally Malthus would have been interested to learn that in the United States and probably also in the Soviet Union there are now waiting enough hydrogen bombs to erase the inhabitants of a large part of the world and poison the natural resources of the few who might be left.

Aside from war, natural resources difficult to restore are being used in large-scale production, both in the United States and in other parts of the world. Does our planning take into account that unless we economize in these resources our wealth may disappear? Do we really need space ships circumnavigating the ionosphere or landing on the moon or Mars? The notion of emigrating to satellites when the world has become overcrowded or when wars threaten the existence of mankind is popular with the authors of science fiction, but it does not belong among serious projects for the human future.

At present our economists are occupied with more immediate questions, and they have had an encouraging degree of success in finding answers. The detailed picture of the United States economy and the advice concerning economic policy contained in one year's *Economic Report* are outstanding examples of guided planning in an economic regime in which private enterprise and governmental service both play an important role. But new situations and new policies are likely to need attention as our society develops year by year. Let us look briefly at some of those situations.

The national economic reports already issued have concentrated attention on the industries producing tangible goods and have emphasized the growth of productivity in the manufacture of those goods. Yet in recent years the fraction of the population employed in the service industries, which do not produce goods, has become larger than the fraction employed in production. Some of the service occupations are wholesale and retail trade, communications, education, services of professional men, governmental administration, production of literature and the fine arts, "do-it-yourself" work in homes, philanthropy, and the like. Output per man or per man-hour in service occupations is difficult if not impossible to measure. Quality of the output of services is usually more important than increase of output. Should we measure the contribution of education by the number of students graduated per teacher? Should we measure the fine arts by the number of paintings or musical compositions completed per artist or per composer? Should we assess the efficiency of courts of law by the number of convictions or acquittals? Or, in those fields, should the economists abandon any attempt at quantitative measurement?

Another developing situation not stressed in the economic reports to the President is the fact that in recent years between 60 and 70 per cent of all expenditures of the federal government have gone to military defense and related fields. To cite one example, the estimate of the federal budget for the fiscal year 1966 showed that, with a total expenditure of $99,687 million, $51,578 million would go to national defense,[1] $5100 million would be spent on space research and technology, and $4623 million on veterans' benefits and services. Thus $61,301 million, or more than three-fifths of the budget, was connected with warfare, present or past. That sum might be compared with the expenditure for education—$2663 million; commerce and transportation—$2804 million; natural resources (including water)—$2691 million; international affairs and finance—$3984 million; housing and community development—$10 million (not $10 billion); and even health, labor, and welfare—$8328 million.

Gains of the civilian economy are not due to military expenditures, as many suppose. On the contrary, large military spending has made necessary higher taxes (since deficits in the federal budget have been relatively small), while war industries have deprived the civilian economy of the services of many competent

[1] This figure of $51,578 million rose to $56,560 million and $60,541 million, respectively, in the budget estimates for the two succeeding fiscal years. Of course the rising figures reflected the cost of the war in Vietnam.

executives, scientists, and wage-earners. If disarmament could be safely achieved, the individual consumers could have much more to spend than at present and more to buy with their spending, as well as having more leisure.

A final situation not discussed in the economic reports—and for obvious reasons—has to do with the politics of economic planning. During the twenty years that followed World War II, planning has led to the timely application of such measures as increased government spending, reductions in the tax rate, and tax credits for business construction, all with the aim of increasing the rate of expansion of the economy. Expansion is always popular. As a matter of practical politics, the question is whether the machinery of planning can be operated equally well in reverse. When business expansion becomes too rapid or when the public has more dollars than available goods to spend them for, can we put a brake on speculative investment and dizzily rising prices? In theory there is no difficulty whatever: simply by raising taxes and lowering its expenditures, the government can bring the economy back to a steadier rate of growth. In practice, however, there are formidable obstacles to this course. There is the danger, for example, that the remedies might prove too drastic and that a sudden change in the government's balance sheet might lead to a sharp recession. There is the quite natural resistance of the public to higher taxes. There is the fact, moreover, that any government appropriation continued over a series of years creates a powerful business and administrative interest that will fight against having the appropriation reduced or ended.

The situation is likely to become critical in an election year. In the spring of 1966, for example, economists were in general agreement that prices were rising too fast and that measures should be taken to reduce the "overheating," as they called it, of the economy. Most of the inflationary pressure resulted from the fighting in Vietnam, but there was also a rise in civilian demand for consumer goods. Higher taxes would have reduced the demand, though they might have been politically inexpedient. In any case the administration did not propose that obvious remedy. Another inflationary factor was the rise in business spending for building, machinery, and equipment. Private enterprise had been encouraged to spend by a 7-per-cent tax credit for new investment. Would the administration take the necessary step of recommending that the tax credit be suspended? After hesitating all through the summer, it finally submitted a bill that was passed by Congress, but only after prices had risen to a dangerous level. A probable, though never officially recognized, reason for the delay was that loss of tax credits might lead to loss of business support and that a new Congress was being elected in November.

The situation presents a problem to planners that might be solved in the future by more courage on the part of legislators and administrators and a wider public knowledge of economic principles. Meanwhile we can look with some degree of pride at the record of economic planning in the United States since World War II. It has contributed to a steady increase in the national product as well as to a nationwide decrease in poverty, and it has avoided postwar calamities like the collapse of the economy in the 1930s. It has done this, moreover, without economic dictatorship by the government. Unlike Russian Soviet planning it has never abandoned private enterprise; and it has encouraged competition except in the cases where public utilities were regulated in the interest of consumers. Its results have been obtained by careful analysis of economic trends and by continual discussion among governmental economists, business executives, and labor leaders. The method followed, that of a free society, is in itself an honorable achievement.

Further Reading

Beard, Charles A. and Mary R. *The Rise of American Civilization.* 2 vols. New York: Macmillan, 1927.

Berle, Adolph A., Jr. *The 20th Century Capitalist Revolution.* New York: Harcourt, 1954.

Faulkner, Harold U. *The Decline of Laissez-Faire, 1897-1917.* New York: Rinehart, 1951.

Federal Reserve System, Board of Governors. *Purposes and Functions,* 1954.

Goodrich, Carter (ed.). *Canals and American Economic Development.* New York: Columbia University Press, 1961.

Keynes, John Maynard. *The Economic Consequences of the Peace.* New York: Harcourt, 1920.

Kirkland, Edward Chase. *Men, Cities, and Transportation: A Study in New England History, 1820-1900.* 2 vols. Cambridge: Harvard University Press, 1948.

————. *Industry Comes of Age: Business, Labor, and Public Policy, 1860-1897.* New York: Holt, 1961.

Kuznets, Simon. *National Income and Its Composition, 1919-1938.* New York: The National Bureau of Economic Research, 1941.

Soule, George. *Prosperity Decade: From War to Depression, 1917-1929.* New York: Rinehart, 1947.

Stocking, George W., and Watkins, Myron W. *Monopoly and Free Enterprise.* New York: The Twentieth Century Fund, 1951.

Wallace, Donald H. *Economic Controls and Defense.* (With a chapter by J. M. Clark on basic problems and policies.) New York: The Twentieth Century Fund, 1953.

Index

Adams, John Quincy, 27
Agenbeguan (Soviet economist), 165
Agricultural Adjustment Act (1933), 113, 118, 168
Agricultural Adjustment Act (1938), 118-19
Agricultural Adjustment Administration (AAA), 110, 118, 123, 137, 138
Agricultural Marketing Act (1929), 79
Agriculture, 5-6, 14, 24-25, 156; products of, 137, 139; prosperity of, 34, 43-44, 56, 59, 62, 75, 86, 119-20; U.S. policies regarding, 78-79, 98, 113, 117-20; in U.S.S.R., 162-64, 165
Allies, financing of World War I, 37, 42
American Economic Association, 82
American Federation of Labor, 45, 95
"American Plan," 52
American Revolution, 20, 22, 23, 25
Anti-trust laws, 31, 48, 63, 120, 152-153, 167; see also Monopoly
Appalachian Regional Commission, 157
Area Redevelopment Act (1961), 157
Articles of Confederation, 20, 25
Austria, 103, 166

Baker, Newton D., 53
Balance of international payments, 69-70, 96, 117, 154, 169
Bank of England, 75
Bank of the United States, 21, 22
Banking: central, 71; foreign, 75, 83, 103; in U.S., 21-22, 48, 67-68, 76, 101-102, 105-108, 110-11, 114, 126, 131, 132, 134-35, 140
Baruch, Bernard, 42
Beard, Charles A., 95
Belgium, 166
Berle, Adolph, 109
Bimetallism, 23
Blue eagle, 121
Board of Economic Warfare, 140
Bonds: foreign government, 37; U.S. government, 38, 40, 54, 73-74, 127, 134-35, 140
Brandeis, Louis D., 123-24
Budget, U.S.: balanced, 62, 81-82, 84, 98, 124; size of, 96, 112, 126-27, 130-31, 132, 151
Bureau of Labor Statistics, 22
Burns, Arthur F., quoted, 153-54
Business: and U.S. society, 56-57, 131-32; welfare and profits of, 34, 39, 40, 56-58, 61, 64, 86, 120, 140, 150; see also Expansion, business; Production, industrial

Canada, 166
Canals, 28
Capitalism, 3, 8, 9, 18, 25, 62, 98-101, 123-24
Chamber of Commerce, 95
Charity, private, 85, 86; see also Public relief
Chase, Stuart, 95
City planning, 158
Civil Rights Act (1964), 157
Civil Works Administration, 112
Civilian Conservation Corps (CCC), 112
Clark, J. M., 40